Unspoken Loss: Men, Infidelity, and Disenfranchised Grief

—⁓—

Dr. Elliott Kronenfeld, LICSW, CSTS

Unspoken Loss: Men, Infidelity, and Disenfranchised Grief, published June, 2025

Editorial and proofreading services: Beth Raps; Gina Sartirana
Interior layout: Howard P. Johnson
Cover: Artwork by Dimitrios Gripeos; Cover design by Howard P. Johnson
Photo credits: Author photo by Adriana Kopinja
Rendered figures designed by Dimitrios Gripeos and owned by Elliott
Kronenfeld, Ph.D., LICSW, CSTS

SDP Publishing

Published by SDP Publishing, an imprint of SDP Publishing Solutions, LLC.

To obtain permission(s) to use material from this work, please submit an email request with subject line: SDP Publishing Permissions Department.
Email: info@SDPPublishing.com.

ISBN-13 (print): 979-8-9922388-4-6
ISBN-13 (ebook): 979-8-9922388-5-3

Library of Congress Control Number: 2025908419

DEDICATION

To the men brave enough to share their stories
and their loved ones that were able to love them
through their growth.

ACKNOWLEDGMENTS

The greatest gratitude to the men who participated in my study and shared such vulnerable and intimate stories of the lowest times in their lives. Your ability to speak your truth will help so many. Watching you grow from vulnerability and honesty is at once humbling and humanistic.

To the men and couples who have come to my office to work through the pain of their infidelities in the hope of finding a more grounded future, my appreciation for your trust in me and the intensity of the work you have done is limitless. I am deeply inspired by your ability to face great personal fracture with commitment and desire for a better way—and your working toward that. You inspire me every day.

A huge thank you to Tiane Jennings, Miri Skolnik, and Eric-Paul Olsson for the time, insight, and support you've given this writing. Your feedback and reactions were priceless.

Michelle Marzullo, Aaron Norton, and Vicki Shemin your support for my study and understanding why looking at this challenging issue was important has allowed me to help so many. Your guidance and gentle hand have allowed me to be a better clinician, teacher, and advocate.

This book is a team effort. Dimitrios Gripeos, Beth Raps, Gina Sartirana, Howard P. Johnson, Lisa Akoury-Ross, and the team from SDP have allowed this book writing process to be a complete joy. Thank you for pushing, pulling, critiquing, and celebrating.

Joe, Michael, and Olivia – you are always the foundation for everything I do in life.

TABLE OF CONTENTS

Part 3: INTERVENTION 141

FOREWORD

Meeting Elliott Kronenfeld for dinner almost a decade ago at the best Chinese restaurant in town marked my memorable introduction to him. Breaking the ice in these awkward situations is never easy—who is going to order what? What are the boundaries? Are we each ordering for ourselves, or are we expected to share?

Ever the thoughtful gentleman, Elliott asked me what I was thinking. I told him I was having a hard time deciding because everything looked so tempting. At that moment the waiter came over to ask if we were ready to order appetizers; reading my mind, Elliott pronounced—"please bring the pu pu platter!" He intuitively knew that mini-smorgasbord would be a win-win.

That simple beginning tells you everything you need to know about Elliott: he looks out for everyone who has a seat at the table, and he approaches all things with directness and curiosity. (Well, you should also know he has the best collection of eyeglasses in the tri-state area, which I have come to think of as augmenting his gift of seeing what is difficult for others to envision—multidimensionally and in a new light.)

Not long thereafter, I was mesmerized when Elliott gave his extraordinary TEDx Talk at the John F. Kennedy Presidential Library and then shared in his delight when his first book, *Couples by Intention,* was published. But my journey with Elliott did not end there as I was honored to be one of his Ph.D. dissertation advisors. Having worked closely with him in that role over the course of many months, it seems only a natural progression that his doctoral labor of love expanded its roots and branched out to become this, his amazing second book.

In the years since that dinner, Elliott and I have made cross-referrals in the hopes that we could help clients navigate more holistically the treacherous transition from being in a relationship to legally separating. In my role as a family law practitioner and in his role as therapist, we had the same philosophical commitment to convey to clients, in theory and practice, that we honored each not as a "case" but as individuals who deserved nothing less than the best we could offer.

Notably, although our specializations have many areas of overlap, as a divorce attorney, my day-to-day professional work is at the opposite end of the spectrum from Elliott's focus. And yet Elliott is not surprised to know that, because of my clinical social work background, the first question I ask couples is what they may have done to work on their relationship before calling a lawyer's office: this is critically important because, as Elliott emphasizes, infidelity, despite its pain and complexity, does not have to be the end of the line for couples. Being anything but Pollyannaish about what it takes to do the difficult and sometimes excruciatingly unbearable healing work in the aftermath of infidelity, and being acutely sensitive to the landmine of triggering retraumatization, in this book, Elliott holds out a vision for a hopeful future to which couples can strive and attain, albeit with the recognition that the road will be long and predictably fraught with, and impeded by, setbacks.

I concur with Elliott's hunch that, if you are reading this book, you are probably (i) a man who has been unfaithful, (ii) a partner betrayed, or (iii) a clinician working with a man or couple with the goal of helping them heal and grow from the emotional fracture caused by the infidelity. And yet, if none of those apply, you will absolutely benefit from reading the book by gaining deep empathy and a rich understanding—beyond a mere prurient "Bravolebrity" interest as to "who did what to whom and when"—about what countless millions of couples wrestle with each day. Adding another readership category to Elliott's hunch: in the world of divorce, it is incumbent upon legal practitioners to inform themselves about the complex dynamics of infidelity in the hope that perhaps opting for divorce upon learning of an infidelity is not the wisest course in the long-term (especially because, as Elliott reflects, this is all too often a knee-jerk reaction).

It is rare to come across a book that will satisfy the most ardent academics while also appealing to anyone who has ever been part of a family or in a relationship, for this book is eminently readable and relatable. But that is the essence of Elliott's superpower—taking his years of acquired professional and anecdotal wisdom and distilling it into care and humanity for each client and for each couple who is lucky enough to have worked with him. Since no one professional could accommodate all the millions of people to whom this book will appeal, these pages will be the next best thing. The case studies create a feeling that one is virtually in the therapeutic treatment room and reveal how diverse the experiences of infidelity are even while the uniqueness of each story is counterbalanced with universal themes.

To inculcate in us the phenomenon of infidelity, Elliott tackles the complex subject matter by dividing the book into three parts: Theory and Gaining an Understanding of Infidelity, Research, and Intervention. Although the research can be an interesting launching point, Elliott understands that the reader will first want more context and he brilliantly delivers on this. Paralleling what couples who have experienced infidelity have undergone, readers will find themselves on the same emotional, whirlwind rollercoaster endured by those couples. You will feel like you are sitting in the clinician's room observing the work first-hand because these experiences are recounted in such exquisite and compassionate detail. Along the way, you will come to know intimately the case studies of men and couples Elliott has either treated or who have been part of his research. Elliott invites us to bear witness to their personal stories, struggles, and realities to understand what worked, and maybe more importantly, what did not work, to help propel couples forward in recovery.

And who better than Elliott to plumb the depths of this delicate topic? An expert on how men navigate infidelity recovery, Elliott developed and launched a national study to pull the curtain back on men who sought treatment in connection with their infidelity. In digestible terms for both academic and lay readers alike, he has shone a light on "disenfranchised grief" – the unacknowledged or invalidated emotions men often experience when they are seen as the betrayer without sufficient attention given to their own emotional pain.

One aspect of the book that particularly resonated with me professionally involves what I call "the Greek chorus" of seemingly well-meaning family, friends, and colleagues, who may, consciously or subconsciously, stand quite apart from being a healthy support system. Elliott brings this dynamic into sharp focus by cautioning that "your story can truly only be told over time based on the work ... put into healing." This is but one kernel of wisdom the reader will appreciate in this book.

The "arc of infidelity recovery" is a perfect bespoke term to guide the reader through the various phases. In our everyday parlance and in literature, we think of an arc as a continuous part of a circle that is dynamic, moving, and growing, all as part of a continuing storyline. The points along Elliott's clinical arc start with "crisis," when both partners feel overwhelmed and their thinking and judgment are cloudy. This is typically a time when a divorce lawyer's phone may ring; however, we should be mindful of considering whether it is appropriate to redirect clients to therapy for guidance and further exploration before pulling the plug on the relationship. The crisis is typically triggered by a partner's discovery, or the man's disclosure, of the affair. Long-carried secrets see the light of day and a tsunami ensues. At a sink-or-swim for many couples, those who opt for therapy can feel like this is a lifeline.

The next point in the arc is "keeping vigil and regrounding," apt descriptions as they convey how fragile a state the relationship is in at that juncture, often teetering on the edge of extinction. Moving to "reconnecting" in the aftermath of the infidelity is a point on the arc during which it is hoped the couple can achieve what Elliott calls "functional stasis." If the couple can navigate forward to the next points on the arc, then "retrusting" and "forward planning" can be achieved, being ever mindful that trust is a choice all along the path of the arc.

In the end, we would all do well to heed the wisdom of Elliott's grandmother, Anna: "Do your work now, or do your work later. Eventually you will have to do the work and the longer you wait, the harder it is."

As mentioned, Elliott's superpower is his directness and curiosity that has enabled him to venture into frontiers where many dare not tread to do the hard work and to elevate the profession and our society by so doing. Anna would be proud of the hard work her grandson Elliott has done to, in turn, help those who have experienced infidelity journey forward, heal, and be their best selves.

— VICKI L. SHEMIN, J.D., LICSW, ACSW, is a family law attorney and clinical social worker at Fields and Dennis, LLP in Wellesley, Massachusetts. Recognized by The Best Lawyers in America®and SuperLawyers®, she has devoted her four-decade career to helping families attain peaceful and collaborative resolutions. She is working on a book entitled "Letters to Ex-Spouses: …And I Just Wanted You to Know."

PREFACE

This book, by its very nature and subject, is challenging to write and may be even more challenging to read! Exploring and talking about infidelity is never an easy topic and never one someone takes up just out of pure curiosity. It is my assumption that if you are reading this book you are probably one of three people: a man who committed infidelity in your relationship; a partner who was betrayed in your relationship; a clinician working with the man or the couple to help them heal and grow from such an emotional blow to their relationship.

If you are none of these, I hope you are reading this book with an openness to learning because the issues approached in the coming chapters are often ones that take on a new meaning once you have lived the experience.

Infidelity is challenging to understand from a purely academic perspective without grounding it in the human realities that must be navigated. As such, this book is structured in a very particular way. First, it is important to know some core theoretical perspectives and the research that has been done to date to better understand the phenomenon of infidelity: what it is, why it happens, some of the statistics, and what researchers know about it. It is not uncommon, once an infidelity is discovered or disclosed, that a flood of questions burst forth. This is why I present what is known at this time *first*. I intend Part One of the book to give you a fresh framework for understanding your experience (if you are part of a couple that has been impacted by infidelity) or your clients' experience (if you are a clinician). Without this framework and structure, just talking about what you or your partner are going through risks retraumatizing you, creating new blame, or missing foundational pieces that allow healing to happen. You can certainly jump ahead in the book and read parts that feel the most critical, too, but I recommend—at some point early in the healing process—that you read the beginning chapters.

I also feel it is important to note that no two infidelities are alike. When you hear from friends, families, coworkers, or others about how infidelity has impacted them, don't make their story yours, and don't let them tell you how your story will turn out. Your story can truly only be told over time based on the work you both put into healing.

Couples will often attempt to work through the infidelity on their own, or sometimes, only one partner will go to therapy. I don't know the right course of healing for everyone; however, it has been my experience that it is the rare couple who break down the dynamics, understand the precursors, and craft the conversations and boundaries that allow for real growth to emerge out of the devastation of infidelity without working with professional counselors experienced in working with these issues. Find the professionals early. Find the people that you can work with who hold the hope of recovery with you and your partner.

⁓

A note before you dive in: while every infidelity is unique, I often group them into two categories based on underlying dynamics.

The first category involves men who lose their way within their primary relationship, often during times of emotional disconnect or relational stress. This form of infidelity is driven by a man's inability to address dissatisfaction, loneliness, or unmet needs within the relationship. It is not uncommon for these men to seek relief outside their relationship. In these cases, it's essential to remember that infidelity doesn't happen in a vacuum—there are often underlying relational dynamics that contribute to the betrayal. The affair may be a misguided attempt to find emotional validation or connection that has been missing from the relationship, although it never justifies the harm caused.

The second category involves men who have developed a recurring pattern of behavior that exists outside of their primary relationship. This type of infidelity is often marked by compulsive or habitual actions that can stem from deeper issues, such as unresolved emotional struggles, sexual compulsivity, or an inability to manage personal boundaries. For these cases, I recommend reading *Treating Out of Control Sexual Behavior* by Doug Braun-Harvey and Michael Vigorito. Their work provides an in-depth look at how to understand

and treat these behaviors in a way that fosters personal responsibility and self-regulation, helping men to break these destructive cycles.

The book you are reading focuses on the first category.

✑

In closing, when I am doing infidelity recovery work, I am very clear in the first session that this relationship is over. It is a devastating thing to hear, and clients have a strong reaction to that flash of truth. I follow it up with a question: "Do you want your next relationship to be with this person? If so, our work is focused on what that new relationship needs to be and how it will be different from your former relationship. We will keep what worked and learn from what did not, but the goal is not to go back to the broken relationship and try to recreate what you had when you thought it was great. That is impossible to do. What happens next is you move into a new and healthier relationship based on new knowledge, skill, and commitments."

Last, to quote one of the smartest people I ever met, my Grandmother Anna, "Do your work now, or do your work later. Eventually you will have to do the work and the longer you wait, the harder it is."

PART

I

THEORY AND GAINING AN UNDERSTANDING OF INFIDELITY

❧

Healing from infidelity requires embracing vulnerability and allowing yourself to feel.

—Author Unknown

INTRODUCTION

Infidelity is a deeply personal and often taboo topic in our society—a violation of trust that can shake the very foundation of relationships. Cheating—in any form—is one of the few relationship topics that is still not talked about in the broader society because it is painful and laden with deep judgments for all involved. The breach of infidelity can happen in seemingly strong and healthy relationships; this feeds the shock and awe when it happens.

Infidelity comes from the root word "fidelity" which means loyalty or trust. So, infidelity is anything that breaks trust or creates a sense of disloyalty. It can be sexual, emotional, financial, social, and include several other infractions. While much attention has been rightfully given to the experiences of betrayed partners, the emotional landscape of those who *commit* infidelity remains largely uncharted. Society is often quick to demonize the perpetrators who create such a breach.

The purpose of this book is to better understand the betrayer's perspective—what leads to infidelity and how the ultimate discovery or disclosure of such a breach is experienced without offering a free pass or excuse for such behavior. While infidelity can happen in good relationships, and there are many precursors to infidelity, ultimately we are all responsible for the choices we make and must address the reality of those outcomes.

In the realm of relationships and infidelity, when dominant narratives focus on the betrayed partner's experience, there is little room for the complex realities faced by those who commit infidelity. Particularly overlooked are heterosexual men, whose perspectives and emotional journeys are frequently misunderstood or sidelined in both scholarly research and social representation. In an age where patriarchy and male dominance are openly challenged, the experiences of these men are often assumed and prejudged without a true sense of the foundational building blocks that helped to create them.

This book delves into the complexities of *why* men commit infidelity, aiming to understand their experiences and the factors that drive them to cheat, as well as what their experience of the recovery and healing process is like. It is important to note that my exploration is not meant to provide a "Get Out of Jail Free" card or excuse their actions. Instead, my goal is to shed light on the underlying issues, emotional struggles, and societal pressures that contribute to infidelity. Again, understanding the reasons for infidelity doesn't absolve the offender of responsibility or dissolve the pain caused by their betrayal but offers a more nuanced path to growth and understanding that is at the same time both more realistic and more healing. By gaining this deeper understanding, we avoid the trap of black-and-white thinking and can address these factors more effectively and foster healthier, more honest relationships and a more meaningful recovery process.

Men who cheat must own their decisions and actions, taking full responsibility for the hurt and betrayal they have caused. The goal of this book is to create a path forward that addresses the needs of both the betrayed partner and the man who committed the infidelity. It's about fostering open communication, rebuilding trust, and healing the wounds on both sides—and yes, both sides are hurt! Understanding the reasons behind the infidelity is just one part of the process; the real work lies in repairing the relationship and ensuring that both partners feel heard, valued, and supported as they navigate the difficult journey of reconciliation and growth.

I am aware that men and women alike can commit acts of infidelity, yet acknowledge that the experiences can differ significantly due to socialization, gendered expectations, and power dynamics inherent in heterosexual relationships. Additionally, LGBTQ+ partners can be deeply challenged in the face of infidelity; however, there are significant and unique social realities and challenges for this community as they navigate the constructions of their relationships and the fractures they experience. It is for these reasons this book is focused on cisgender, heterosexual men. It would be a disservice to globalize the research findings and experiences to other populations without looking at the unique factors in different types of relationships.

How This Book Works

This book seeks to shine a light on the nuanced and often uncharted territory of men who have committed infidelity and how they experience and understand the impacts on their partners, themselves, and others. It challenges the prevailing notion that infidelity is solely a matter of betrayal and victimhood, recognizing instead that both partners in a relationship can experience profound hurt, confusion, and emotional injury. This book delves into the multifaceted experiences of men grappling with infidelity and its aftermath. When you cruise the bookshelves looking for help to overcome infidelity, most books (as well as most social media) tend to focus on the betrayed partner's perspective, leaving a significant gap in understanding the complexities faced by the men who have strayed. This book aims to fill that gap by exploring the emotional landscapes, challenges, and personal growth journeys of these men.

This book also seeks to explore a side of infidelity that is seldom discussed: the disenfranchised grief experienced by the betrayed partners as well as the men who find themselves on the other side of fidelity. Infidelity, which frequently occurs in secrecy, is often a deeply traumatic experience for all parties for very different reasons. Each partner must heal from different emotional injuries. For too long, the conversations surrounding infidelity have been polarized into victims and perpetrators, casting individuals into rigid roles that fail to capture the complexity of human emotion and experience. Behind closed doors, many men who have engaged in infidelity grapple with profound feelings of guilt, shame, and sorrow—emotions that are often stifled by social scripts defining masculinity and the fear of public and private judgment. This is how grief becomes "disenfranchised": disenfranchised grief is grief that cannot be spoken or expressed for fear of retribution and increased judgment. By exploring how disenfranchised grief manifests in men who commit infidelity, this book provides a nuanced perspective on the emotional toll and complexities of navigating this guilt, shame, and remorse while on the journey to healing.

Through personal stories, psychological insights, and social analysis, we will look at the multifaceted journey of men who have committed infidelity. The book challenges conventional stories and invites readers to consider the often misunderstood experiences that accompany the actions of these men. By better understanding the intersection of infidelity and disenfranchised grief in men, we begin to understand that recovery from infidelity must be more holistic, balanced, and incorporate more complex dialogues while each partner does their own work of healing.

I have included interviews, research findings, and therapeutic perspectives that uncover the internal conflicts these men face as they navigate the aftermath of their choices and behaviors. I explore how infidelity can represent a loss not only of relationships but also of self-identity, integrity, and personal values. This loss is made more complex by the stigmas that discourage open discussion and healing. As men grapple with cultural expectations of masculinity, gender roles, and norms, which are created through the ways in which young boys are socialized and instructed to behave, feel, and communicate as they grow into men, it becomes clear why infidelity recovery is such a deeply complex journey. Men are not groomed to talk about deep feelings, show weakness, talk about relationship dissatisfaction while naming their faults in meaningful ways—and the research study that will be presented in this book brings forward the impacts of this on both relationship partners.

This book also examines the ripple effects of infidelity on personal well-being, relationships, and broader social dynamics. It confronts the isolation and loneliness that often accompany disenfranchised grief, offering insights into how men can begin to reconcile their actions, heal emotional wounds, and forge a path toward personal growth and redemption while trying to support their partner through their unique path to healing. Also included are the impacts on children and family members, friends, work, and the greater community. Infidelity never happens in a vacuum.

This journey also includes a direct and clear look at how therapy processes work and don't work for people seeking relief from infidelity. Through extensive research and direct clinical experience, I have included specifics on what makes for meaningful therapy for men individually and for couples trying to untwist the knots that infidelity creates. It is important to note that infidelity recovery is a clinical specialty and recovery is best supported by engaging with practitioners with a deep well of knowledge and experience.

Ultimately, this is a book about empathy, understanding, and wholeness—a call to expand our empathy beyond the roles of victim and perpetrator and to acknowledge the complex emotional realities faced by all parties involved in the aftermath of infidelity. It challenges us to reconsider our assumptions about fidelity, masculinity, and the capacity for transformation and resilience in the face of profound emotional turmoil. By validating and exploring the experiences of men who have committed infidelity, it encourages readers to engage in deeper reflections on relationships, personal integrity, and the complexity of human emotions. Using deep curiosity and intentionality, readers can begin to question their own experiences, expectations, and what they think a healthy relationship looks like.

The foundation of this exploration is a rigorous research study I conducted as a Ph.D. in Human Sexuality and certified sex therapist specializing in infidelity recovery. My national study, which I discuss in depth in Chapters 3 and 6, looked at how men who committed acts of infidelity talked about their experiences before, during, and after discovery or disclosure as they tried to journey back to a stable and healthy relationship. Drawing on years of clinical experience and expertise, I examine how cultural norms, gender roles, standard therapeutic approaches, and expectations of masculinity shape the experiences of men navigating infidelity recovery. Using theoretical frames such as feminist, hegemonic masculinity, and social exchange theories, the realities for men who have committed acts of infidelity will be examined. Also included are the roles individual and couples' therapists, 12-step programs, and other interventions play during the recovery process. This perspective is crucial in unpacking the complexities of emotional turmoil, identity reconstruction, and relationship dynamics that emerge in the wake of infidelity. These factors set the opportunities and limitations these men identify for themselves, their partners, and their hopeful futures.

It is important to clarify that while this book acknowledges the existence and validity of consensual nonmonogamy, its focus remains on relationships where monogamy was presumed. Furthermore, the book explores the often-overlooked scenario where both partners in a relationship have committed acts of infidelity, albeit possibly at different times, as retribution, or of different types. There is also the consideration where one partner engages in behaviors they believe are within the bounds of the relationship but which the partner sees as infidelity. This recognition challenges simplistic stories of blame and victimhood, inviting a deeper understanding of the complexities within relationships.

Much of the infidelity that I treat has occurred in perceivably healthy relationships. If infidelity is understood as both a covert behavior and a desire or pleasure that does not center on the primary partner, there can be an immediate judgment that the entire relationship is faulty and a sham. This is often not true. There is an instinct by the betrayed partner, in their shock and hurt, to name the entire relationship as broken and dishonest. There are many instances when most of the relationship is working and meaningful and both partners must reengage to assess what parts of the relationship are working and where change must happen. While infidelity can sometimes be a passive way of exiting the relationship, I find that this is not frequently the case. I find rather that the decision the partners must make is whether to stay together, working on reconnecting and healing the emotional injuries while restructuring the relationship to be more functional.

When we can approach the story of infidelity with curiosity, even in the face of deep pain, we get richer and more meaningful stories, and ultimately more meaningful recovery. Whether you are a man who committed an act of infidelity, his betrayed partner, a therapist looking for deeper understanding, or another impacted person, this book should bring you insight.

Chapter

1

▾

THE BASICS OF INFIDELITY

If you are reading this book, it is likely that you have impacted your relationship by an act of infidelity, your partner has done so, both of you have impacted your relationship in this way, or you are in a supportive role for a person or relationship reeling from the betrayal. Regardless of the reason you are reading, it is important to name what we know about the deeply impactful experience of infidelity. In this chapter, we will explore common social narratives about it, take a quick look at what the research says, and name some of the significant questions it's common to have about it. Infidelity is a complex experience and no two betrayals are the same.

Our goal in exploring these things is to explore the social and cultural understandings that surround infidelity, address misconceptions, open up curiosity about human behavior, and increase our capacity for reflection. No book can cover the entirety of the experience of infidelity and its impact: it is too vast, too varied, too complex, and too personal. No one book will answer all the questions, give all the insights, or supply all the comfort and relief that are needed. Hopefully, however, this book *will* provide a substantial amount of all that as a stepping stone in the journey to healing from infidelity.

HOW WE THINK ABOUT INFIDELITY

▼ He's different ... I got a good one!

▼ He loves me so much that he would never ...

▼ He knows I have been hurt before ...

▼ Once a cheater, always a cheater!

▼ You have no integrity or morals ... just pathetic!

▼ If you ever cheat, the relationship is over!

▼ You cheated because you are addicted to porn and sex!

Think about all the messages about infidelity we get from friends, family, faith, and media as we are growing up.

There are so many aspirational and idealized messages about love and connection. There are also so many warnings about trust, love, and betrayal, yet we often believe that our relationship will be different.

We hear stories of infidelity and think, "that won't happen to me," because we trust our partners and the bond we have built, as well as an often false sense of our own ability to identify and get in front of anything that might open the door to such pain.

But if infidelity does happen, it's a harsh reminder that those warnings weren't just empty words. It makes us question everything we ever believed about love, connection, our partners, and the bond we have built, leaving us to piece together a new understanding of our relationship—and ourselves.

Beliefs about infidelity—and who is at fault—have deep, entrenched roots. In the 1949 *Handbook for Husbands,* for instance, readers were warned that most divorces are initiated by wives, with the blame commonly placed on the husband, often due to "another woman." The same manual advised wives to "accept" their sexual responsibilities, implying that a woman's duty was to meet her husband's needs without question while disregarding her own. Although our understanding of healthy marriages and the dynamics of fidelity have evolved significantly since then, the damaging remnants of these patriarchal beliefs still persist in subtle ways today. Concepts like "sexual duty" and the idea that a spouse's infidelity automatically reflects their partner's shortcomings have left lasting marks on how society perceives commitment and blame in relationships. Ideally, today's perspectives would instead emphasize mutual respect, communication, and shared responsibility. Yet the outdated assumptions still influence the way some couples and society at large grapple with marital conflict and infidelity.

Infidelity is incredibly disorienting because it shakes the very foundation of trust in a relationship. Suddenly, everything that felt stable and real starts to seem fake or questionable. The good times and happy memories are tainted, leaving you wondering if they were ever genuine. It's like a rug being pulled out from under you, leaving you struggling to find your footing and make sense of what was once a solid part of your life. If you had any doubts about the relationship before, infidelity confirms your worst fears and makes you feel like a fool for ignoring the red flags. It's a painful validation of all the uncertainty and unease you felt, amplifying the sense of betrayal and self-doubt.

Prior to experiencing infidelity, it's hard to grasp just how far-reaching the impacts of such a relationship fracture can be. We might imagine it would hurt and cause some trust issues, but the reality is often much deeper and more complex. Infidelity can shake our sense of self-worth, our ability to trust others, and reform our entire worldview. It can seep into every aspect of our lives, from our personal confidence to our future relationships. The emotional fallout can be overwhelming, affecting our mental health, our friendships, and even our professional lives. It's not just about the immediate pain; it's about the long-term process of healing and rebuilding that we can't fully understand until we're in it.

It is also hard to predict how infidelity doesn't just fracture your relationship with your partner; it ripples out and affects your entire network of relations. If you have children, they may sense the tension, confusion, and have an awareness that their parents are not as present and grounded as they were prior—affecting their sense of security and trust. Family gatherings become strained as everyone navigates the emotional fallout, trying to reconfigure what role they should play in the new dynamic while not understanding all of the triggers. Or, in an even more challenging situation, family gatherings can create more distance and isolation if no one has been told about the bomb that just went off in the relationship and everyone is trying to "normalize" dinner. Friends can often feel caught in the middle, unsure how to offer support. Social connections that you once took for granted become complicated as people take sides or create distance so they don't have to engage in the drama. The betrayal disrupts the stability and harmony in all areas of your life, making it challenging to find solace, support, and firm ground when you need it most.

Infidelity can happen in all types of relationships regardless of how strong or perfect they may seem from the outside. It doesn't matter if the couple has been together for a few weeks or several decades, if they are married or just dating, or if they have a traditional or open relationship. Cheating can happen when everything seemed ideal as well as in relationships already facing challenges. The reasons are complex and varied and can affect anyone, regardless of age, background, or circumstances. Infidelity is a universal issue that reminds us that no relationship is immune to difficulties.

Research has found that people who have more dating experience are more likely to have experiences of infidelity and that about 71% of men and 57% of women in dating relationships have experienced some form of infidelity in their dating history (Piercy, Hertlein, and Wetchler). Yet even though infidelity occurs with such frequency, it still catches people off-guard. It's one of those things that you hear happen to others, but when it hits close to home, the shock is real.

Infidelity is often a way for a partner to cope with their dissatisfaction in the relationship without confronting the underlying issues directly. By seeking fulfillment outside the relationship, they might feel a temporary sense of relief or escape from their feelings of unhappiness or disconnection. This secret double life allows them to avoid the difficult conversations and potential conflicts that would come with addressing their dissatisfaction openly. In this way, infidelity becomes a coping mechanism, albeit a destructive one, that enables them to maintain the façade of a stable relationship while hiding their true feelings and unmet needs.

It is important to know that infidelity can happen in even the best relationships where both partners genuinely care for each other and have built a solid foundation of love and trust. It's a common misconception that cheating only occurs in troubled relationships, but the reality is deeply nuanced. Sometimes, external pressures, personal insecurities, or unexpected attractions can lead to infidelity, even when the relationship itself is strong. It's important to understand that a single act of betrayal does not automatically negate all the positive aspects of a relationship.

The reasons behind infidelity are complicated and often have little to do with the quality of the relationship. All relationships require work and all relationships have challenges. However, some individuals cheat due to personal struggles or unresolved issues that they haven't addressed with their partner. They might be seeking validation, excitement, or a distraction from stressors unrelated to the relationship. This doesn't mean their feelings for their partner are any less real or that the relationship itself is inherently flawed. Issues such as work stress or unresolved personal concerns can create emotional vulnerabilities that lead individuals to seek comfort or escape through infidelity, even if they are otherwise happy with their partner. We will learn more about this when we look at infidelity from a theoretical perspective in the next section. Good relationships can face moments of weakness, and infidelity can be a symptom of deeper, individual issues rather than a reflection of the partnership's overall health.

When infidelity happens in a good relationship, it can be traumatic, but it doesn't necessarily mean the relationship is beyond repair. Many couples who face infidelity choose to work through it together, using the experience as a catalyst for growth and deeper understanding. With time, communication, and professional help, partners can rebuild trust and come out stronger on the other side. While the journey to healing is challenging, it's a testament to the resilience and commitment that can exist even in the face of betrayal.

What the Research Says

It is certainly worth our time to look at what is known about infidelity from a research perspective. While each infidelity is unique and leaves both relationship partners feeling isolated and unsupported, knowing the trends and infidelity's greater commonality in society may be helpful. A major part of recovering from infidelity is knowing why and how it happens, what brings people to commit acts of infidelity, and how it is understood across society. Researchers have a variety of conceptual frameworks to help us understand these things.

There is a school of thought that infidelity is influenced by a chemical alchemy of brain hormones and neurotransmitters such as dopamine and norepinephrine (Haltzman; Crenshaw). This research focuses on how these brain chemicals impact mood, brain functioning, and physical sensation when excitement and satisfaction are experienced. When a person initiates an infidelity, the chemical alchemy creates feelings akin to falling in love for the first time. This experience can also deeply impact judgment and reason, challenging decision-making. When a person begins to consider the possibility of infidelity, this chemical soup in the brain begins to make the person feel attractive, swim in the allure of newness, and open up to the possibility of shifts in morality, which creates challenges to executive functioning, and heightened psychiatric disorders—all resulting in an experience that is rife for moving forward with the infidelity.

It would be an incomplete conclusion to think that brain chemistry alone is responsible for infidelity, however. From the biomedical perspective, humans are chemically predisposed to act on impulse and animalistic desire. When desire is present, brain chemicals have powerful control, but this should not discount the importance of social conditions within which human relationships occur. Psychosocial mechanisms such as desired connection, gender performativity, generational expectations, and more must be considered as well. For this reason, this book will explore both the psychosocial as well as the biochemical foundations of infidelity.

A 20-year longitudinal study of 1270 married respondents with no prior stated history of extramarital sex was conducted by a researcher named Alfred DeMaris in 2009. This national study found that up to 25% of adults will experience infidelity, which was the most commonly reported cause of divorce. The longitudinal study determined that the four primary risks for extramarital sex were the personal values of the individual initiating, the opportunity to engage in extramarital sex, the nature of the couple's relationship, and demographic risk factors. These demographic risk factors showed that men are more likely to engage in infidelity due to greater sexual interest, desire for variety, and their ability to separate sex from love. Longer marital duration and higher religiosity were found to be likely to decrease the risks of infidelity due to censure and higher levels of commitment. However, because this study was completed in the first decade of the 2000s, it does not account for rapidly changing societal values or intergenerational evolution in social structures and relationship dynamics.

Exploring the events leading to infidelity, Nicolle Zapien examined the experiences prior to infidelity that might create, allow, or promote the initiation of infidelity. This study looked at relationship dynamics and decision-making, taking into consideration what happens *prior to* an act of infidelity in a relationship. What was discovered are eight core phenomena that precede the initiation of infidelity (76):

1. *Dissatisfaction and hopelessness in the relationship.* The affair is perceived to be something that is in *contrast* to the primary relationship rather than in *addition* to the primary relationship. Additionally, dissatisfaction and hopelessness in the primary relationship are experienced with the belief that no change is possible. The result is the perception that new growth may not be possible so efforts to improve the situation diminish.

2. *Novelty and passion in romantic/sexual relationships.* When novelty and passion—which are believed to be indicative of a healthy relationship—are no longer experienced, dissatisfaction and hopelessness grow.

3. *Deserving sexual satisfaction or intimate connection.* Sexuality and desire are perceived to be foundational to one's identity, and when these are forsaken or denied, a sense of deserving is fostered.

4. *The partner and self are viewed as fixed characters.* When the person who initiates the infidelity views themselves and/or their partner as unwilling or incapable of growth, evolution, and change, no new understandings of the relationship can emerge. This can include the fixed thoughts that one partner is "good" and the other is "bad."

5. *Lack of curiosity for the partner as a subject.* The partner is believed to be rigid, cold, out of touch, and without interest. Lack of curiosity about one's relationship partner reduces the insight that the partner may be equally dissatisfied.

6. *Desire and passion overriding and overtaking one's judgment.* Often when a partner initiates an infidelity, they describe it as something that happened to them, rather than something they orchestrated, directed, and navigated. It is often described as if the experience washed over them rather than their making an intentional, conscious decision.

7. *The affair is not recognized as an affair until after it begins.* There is no clear moment when a partner decides to create

a betrayal. The events leading up to a betrayal are often described as social, playful, or something other than the opening of an infidelity.

8. *Divorce or opening up the relationship are not considered options for resolving the issues.* One of the reasons couples experience infidelity is they are not engaging each other to explore what other relationship structures or experiences should be considered.

While Zapien does not directly identify biochemical brain functioning as a cause of passion and desire overriding judgment, there is some alignment in her study with the idea that the thought processes of the person initiating the infidelity can be out of the norm for them. This implies that in otherwise average settings, when they were not feeling emotionally challenged in their primary relationship, they would consider different choices and perhaps not initiate infidelity.

A third way in which research examines infidelity is the perspective of evolutionary psychology. Evolutionary psychology examines human behavior through the lens of evolution and natural selection, seeking to understand how certain behaviors might have been advantageous for our ancestors' survival and reproduction. It is important to note that some critics of evolutionary psychology argue that it can overemphasize biological determinism and undervalue the influence of culture, socialization, and individual choice. Regarding infidelity, evolutionary psychological researchers have several theories.

A school of researchers (Treger and Sprecher; Cann, Mangum, and Wells) theorize, using evolutionary models, that biology may underlie the sex differences in relationship strategies and responses to relationship fractures. Betrayed men tend to express more distress if their partner has a sexual infidelity, whereas women tend to be more impacted by emotional infidelity. This theory also takes into consideration cross-cultural comparisons of socialization in gender, finding that how individuals conceptualize sex and sexuality prior to infidelity predicts their level of distress.

The evolutionary model of understanding also found a correlation of higher infidelity for men with a partner's pregnancy (Fincham and Beach). There are several theories that explore why this may be true. First, there is a shift in sexual dynamics during pregnancy. For some men, the reduction or alteration in sexual intimacy during pregnancy may be a factor. Second, the woman's emotional and physical needs during pregnancy can be stressful for both partners, leading to physical distance. Third, the man may perceive neglect or feeling less important as the woman's focus shifts to herself and their expected child. This perceived neglect can contribute to feelings of insecurity and inadequacy, sometimes leading to infidelity as a means to regain a sense of importance or validation.

From a social dynamics perspective, how infidelity becomes known is also significant. The experience of disclosure is different than if the betrayed partner is the one who discovers the infidelity. When infidelity is discovered after a period of suspicion, reactions can be intense. Reactions include sadness, violence, sleeplessness, numbness, hyper-alertness, and more. The partner who committed the infidelity is often reluctant to confirm suspicions due to fear of reaction or legal retaliation, desire to protect the affair partner, shame, and fear of losing the primary partner and relationship. When discovery is secretive and happens without prior suspicion, trauma reactions can be intensified. When these trauma reactions are missed or misdiagnosed, additional challenges affect the rebuilding of trust and slow the recovery process (Lusterman). What complicates the recovery process are attempts to hide the core facts of the infidelity after discovery—regardless of the reason—which deepens grief for both parties. One of the most challenging aspects of starting infidelity recovery work is when discovery or disclosure happens in a trickle-down manner or requires the betrayed partner to dig for the story. In this case, I cannot support a couple through the growth and recovery process because there is no starting point for recovery: every day feels like a new day of discovery.

Because existing infidelity research is overwhelmingly heteronormative, it is important to consider the impact on a heterosexual relationship of infidelity with a same-sex affair partner. Given that Judeo-Christian teachings limit sex to marital relations and ground infidelity as a sin, as well as changing social views on same-gender sexual experiences, it is important to consider that an infidelity may not be heterosexual. A 2015 study (Clarke, Braun, and Wooles) looked at the impact of gender in infidelity. Assuming that 25% of heterosexually married people will cheat at some point (men more likely than women), a correlation was found that same-sex infidelity in heterosexual relationships induced less jealousy. However, infidelity between a female partner and a female affair partner was found to be less distressing to a male partner than a male partner committing infidelity with another male was to a female partner.

When a man committed an act of infidelity with another man, the act was seen by the man's female partner as a double dishonesty of infidelity and a countering of the assumed sexual orientation. This finding was written about in Jane Ward's book *Not Gay: Sex Between Straight White Men,* that explores how society is more likely to accept women as sexually fluid if they have sex with another woman, but men are held to strict heteronormative sociosexual rules. Any sexual fluidity for men is seen as a crisis of identity. There is a discounting that a man may enjoy sexual contact with another man in some form without reconsidering his sense of heterosexuality. This concept is becoming more accepted in younger generations but still remains deeply painful for older generations. It is this lack of social awareness that men are just as likely as women to be sexually fluid that makes a same-sex affair more painful. The exposure of perceived "double dishonesty" further complicates recovery for the partner who committed the infidelity. In exploring the basics of infidelity, in closing, it is important to understand that infidelity is not the same for men and for women. When men have infidelities, there is a higher engagement with porn and they are more likely to have multiple one-time partners with sexual intercourse. Conversely, women are more likely to have emotional affairs with fewer partners. However, patterns are changing with changes in social narratives, so that women are increasingly initiating infidelities in a way that closes the gap with men (Zapien).

2
▼

THE CHALLENGE OF MASCULINITY

It is fascinating (and sometimes overwhelming) how dramatically our society has shifted over the past 15 years, and how views on masculinity are being redefined. These days, there is more scrutiny and societal conversation around what it means to be a man. There is a spotlight on the behaviors men exhibit and what is now acceptable. Being a man is no longer just about strength and stoicism. There is a real push for emotional intelligence, empathy, self-awareness, and breaking down old stereotypes. While there is also a resistance to such change, I think it is a positive step toward the development of more grounded, inclusive ideas of masculinity.

The classic messages boys receive—particularly white, cisgender, heterosexual boys—have shaped their self-perception and social expectations. From a young age, they encounter pressure to embody traits like stoicism, strength, and dominance, often at their own self-sacrifice. bell hooks, the noted feminist author and theorist, named this experience plainly when she wrote:

The first act of violence that patriarchy demands of males is not violence toward women. Instead patriarchy demands of all males that they engage in acts of

*psychic self-mutilation, that they kill off the emotional
parts of themselves. If an individual is not successful in
emotionally crippling himself, he can count on patriarchal men to enact rituals of power that will assault his
self-esteem. (66)*

It is this collection of socially imposed thoughts and reactions,
that come not just from patriarchal men but from all of society, that
influence how boys believe they are meant to behave in the world, to
form relationships, and to express themselves emotionally. This pressure can create a complex dynamic where vulnerability is sometimes
viewed as a weakness, leading to internal conflicts about authenticity
and acceptable norms. Navigating these expectations can be challenging as boys and men strive to balance traditional ideals with ever-
evolving concepts of masculinity that open the doors to emotional
openness and empathy. This challenge is deepened when boys and men
lack consistent role models, education, and experiences that support
such openness, vulnerability, and empathy. This journey to reconcile
personal identity with societal expectations can be uniquely challenging for males as they identify and try to integrate their own privilege and expectations into their daily lives.

When men step out of conventional roles and behaviors, it can
create "role strain." Society has clear expectations of what men should
be, how they should act, and what expressions are acceptable. As men
push against these expectations and become less conforming to what is
expected, it can create an intense internal tug-of-war for them. Being
true to oneself often comes at a price of social ridicule, judgment, and
being devalued. With a strong desire to fit in and be acceptable, this
can create a fine tightrope to walk. It becomes a battle of authenticity
against acceptance for many men.

While the challenge of masculinity affects every person on the
planet, there is a different experience for straight white men. In the U.
S., the deep impacts of racism affect how these scripts of masculinity
are interpreted. The expectations of masculinity may shift based on
the racial scripts society imposes on men and boys of color (Curry;
Pascoe). It is important to recognize that men of color have unique
experiences and challenges that cannot be fully captured by research
that focuses primarily on white men. When we lump everyone together
by generalizing about all men based on white men, we overlook the

distinct cultural, social, and historical contexts that shape the lives of men of color. These men often navigate systemic racism, stereotypes, and cultural expectations that affect everything from their mental health to their opportunities in society, from how they experience sexual expectations to how they process emotions, and so much more. Researchers need to dig deeper and consider diverse perspectives if we want to understand the full picture. For this reason, this book focuses on white men. It is important to honor those differences and not globalize the research and clinical approaches discussed in this book. When drawing a distinction is valuable, men of color will be considered in respectful ways.

UNDERSTANDING SCRIPTS

Social scripts are the unwritten rules that guide our interactions and behaviors based on how we think people in different roles should present themselves in various social situations. These scripts are like a tapestry woven from the intersection of the identities of our fore-bears—their histories, eras in which they lived, race, ethnicity, education, faith, immigration status, financial security, political party, birth order, and more. They are also woven from what we have witnessed in our families while we were growing up as well as movies, TV shows, books, social media, and more. All of these factors, or identities, intersect in our own lives, and set a path of expected behaviors and milestones that we—as a new baby—must meet to be considered a successful member of our community. Another way of describing it is as a playbook we all carry around in our minds that tells us how to act, what to say, and how to interpret the actions of others, like invisible hands constantly guiding us.

These scripts are learned through observation, experience, role modeling, and cultural norms from the time we take our first breath. Understanding the scripts or playbooks that guide our lives helps us to understand and appreciate the diversity of human experiences and expectations—even as we challenge and question which scripts we support and which scripts inhibit us.

These scripts guide us at every stage of life and, as bell hooks mentioned in the quotation above, if they are not met, society exacts consequences.

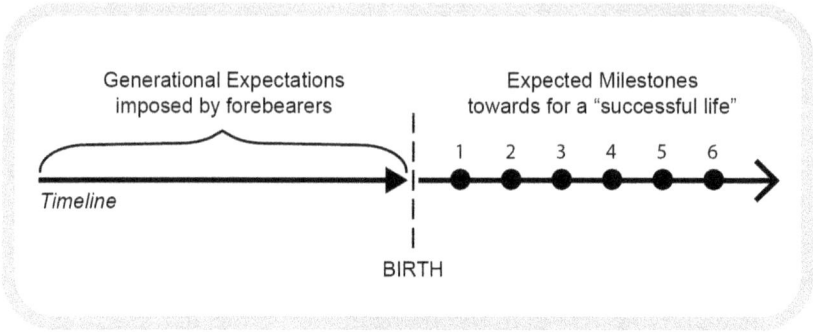

Figure 1: **Social Script Timeline**

These scripts help us navigate complex social landscapes and what is expected of us. We are all deeply affected by this framework as we engage the world around us. No one is immune from such scripts and we often don't acknowledge them until we sense they are problematic or can't live up to them. Often we are not even aware of our scripts as a guiding force that is imposed on us until they are pointed out to us.

Scripts for men begin to frame how men behave, emote, communicate, and understand their roles in relationships. They also affect their partners' expectations. In other words, these scripts tacitly, latently, define the frameworks in which our relationships exist. Very importantly for an understanding of infidelity, it is rare that both partners have the same relationship scripts.

Social scripts also inform us of how we are to understand and perform our sexual selves. The whole topic of sexual behaviors and expectations is deeply layered! Guys grow up with images of what a masculine man looks like by noticing which men get more airtime, which men show up on magazine covers, and the like. These images imprint on young brains.

On top of that, there is the ubiquity of porn, accessible basically everywhere. As porn has become more accessible, the variety and explicitness of it has increased and the younger boys access it, the more imprinting happens. This combination of social messaging and porn can really mess with a guy's understanding of what is expected of him as a man and in a relationship. Understanding his own needs and sexuality and how to behave in a relationship often results in pressured and unrealistic goals that most men can never fulfill. Scripts can create pressure to live up to unrealistic ideals which are tough to navigate when trying to form genuine and authentic connections and understanding healthy sexual relationships.

THREE HELPFUL THEORIES

Three theories help us to better understand how and why men behave the way they do when they commit infidelity. The social scripts mentioned above are a key part of the process but these three theories help us unpack much more. Understanding these theories shines a bright light into the complex labyrinth of men and masculinity. These theories, grounded in research, help us to better see and understand patterns, motivations, and the deeper forces at play behind why men act, think, and feel the ways that they do.

I want to be very clear that my goal in using these theories is not to create stereotypes to box people in but rather to look at commonalities and see patterns that offer insight, learning, and empathy into the complexity of masculinity and how it is expressed. My goal is to move beyond surface-level judgment and appreciate the complex factors that inform masculinity and its presentation through a myriad of factors.

Thus, I share these three theories (which aren't meant to be exhaustive or the final word on masculinity), as a series of three lenses through which we can begin to cultivate curiosity and explore how men develop. Later in the chapter, I show how the lenses can be combined to show us even more, because the three theories sometimes align and support each other, sometimes counter and contradict each other.

Taken together, these theories paint a broader picture of the complex interplay of influences that shape men's development. I invite you to question, critique, and reflect on each of them to see how they expand your knowledge and understanding.

HEGEMONIC MASCULINITY THEORY

The word "hegemonic" refers to something that is dominant, predominant, or exercises authority or influence over others. Hegemonic masculinity theory, originally proposed by sociologist R. W. Connell in the 1980s, offers a framework to understand the dominant form of masculinity within a given cultural context. At its core, hegemonic masculinity refers to the idealized form of masculinity that is culturally and socially dominant, often reinforced through norms, behaviors, and expectations (scripts). This concept acknowledges that within any society, certain traits and behaviors are privileged and seen as the standard for what it means to be a man. These norms not only shape individual identities but also influence power dynamics and social hierarchies.

Central to hegemonic masculinity theory is the idea that masculinity is not actually a fixed or singular identity but rather a dynamic and contested social construct. For example, traits such as physical strength, emotional stoicism, independence, and dominance in social and professional settings are often valorized, while traits that deviate from these norms may be marginalized or stigmatized. Hegemonic masculinity theory emphasizes how different groups of men may strive to conform to or resist the hegemonic idea depending on social, economic, and cultural contexts.

Moreover, hegemonic masculinity theory explores how the dominant form of masculinity is maintained and reproduced (scripted) through various social institutions, including the media, education, politics, and family structures. These institutions play a critical role in perpetuating norms and expectations associated with masculinity, shaping not only the individual behaviors but also the societal attitudes and beliefs of all of the community. Understanding hegemonic masculinity helps to illuminate the complexities of gender dynamics and encourages critical reflection on how gender norms impact individuals and communities within broader social contexts.

Hegemonic masculinity theory sheds light on how society's emphasis on traditional masculine traits can harm women in various ways. When qualities such as aggression, dominance, and emotional suppression are markers of masculinity, it often sets up a power dynamic where men are encouraged to assert control and authority over others, including women. This fosters sexism, gender discrimination in the workplace, violence against women, and more subtle forms like dismissing women's voices, and undervaluing their contributions. In relationships, it often creates barriers for men to express their needs, emotional experiences, and authentic communication, or participate in caregiving roles—things that create stable, trusting, and secure connections.

Hegemonic masculinity can also be deeply harmful to men in a variety of ways. It informs men's health practices, which include difficulty responding to pain and injury, sexual risk-taking, refusing mental health therapies, and ignoring emotional challenges. These attempts to adhere to hegemonic masculinity can result in increased anxiety, depression, emotional distress, the inability to ask for help, and physical pain, as men feel they cannot allow themselves to be vulnerable emotionally, socially, or physically. Conforming to these ideals often leads men to take unnecessary or hurtful risks, behave more aggressively or be more distant and checked-out. Challenges to their masculinity are often perceived as a crisis of identity. Not only do these behaviors harm the men, but they often find their relationships of all types become more strained because they struggle to form deep, emotional connections. Ultimately, the restrictive nature of hegemonic masculinity limits men's ability to live authentically and experience the full range of human emotions and relationships.

It is important here to note that women play a critical role in defining and supporting hegemonic masculinity through their participation in and reinforcement of socially accepted behaviors and expectations that privilege traditional male traits. This process is often subtle and complex, involving a variety of behaviors and attitudes that contribute to maintaining the status quo. First, the greater social forces script how both men and women are to act and distribute influence and power. When women support hegemonic masculinity, it is because of the systems they were raised and socialized in. Just as men are held captive by hegemonic masculinity, so are women. These structures prioritize hegemonic masculinity and then become instrumental in ensuring that such scripts and structures are reinforced.

Socialization and reinforcement: Men and women are socialized into cultural norms from a young age. Parents may reinforce hegemonic masculinity by encouraging traditional gender roles in their children, such as praising boys for being tough and driving them to greater independence and self-sufficiency at a younger age than girls. This reinforcement can happen consciously or unconsciously as men and women internalize these norms and perpetuate them through their expectations and interactions.

Romantic and social expectations: In romantic relationships and social interactions, women might uphold hegemonic masculinity by valuing and rewarding traits associated with traditional masculinity, such as assertiveness, financial success, stoicism, and physical strength and men try to exhibit these behaviors they think makes them more competitive and valuable as they seek partners. Men who display behaviors that deviate from norms, such as emotional expressions of vulnerability or a lower sexual dominance may feel criticized or rejected.

Workplace dynamics: In professional settings, the perpetuation of hegemonic masculinity is supported when employees participate in workplace cultures that valorize traditional gender roles and power dynamics behaviors. In male dominated workplaces, women can struggle to align with these norms to fit in or succeed, inadvertently reinforcing the idea these masculine traits are essential for success while men are getting ahead in greater numbers at a more rapid pace. Furthermore, women in leadership positions might feel pressured to adopt traditionally masculine behaviors to be taken seriously, which can perpetuate the cycle.

Media and cultural representation: Those who work in media, entertainment, and other cultural industries uphold hegemonic masculinity by producing or endorsing content that glorifies traditional masculine ideals. By promoting messages of men as strong, independent, emotionally stoic, and sexually powerful (and women as nurturing, supportive, and desiring of such men), they contribute to the cultural narrative that these are the expected and accepted standards that must be met.

Politics: Women play a role in upholding hegemonic masculinity by aligning with political ideologies and practices that reinforce traditional gender hierarchies. For instance, women may support policies or leaders that emphasize male authority, prioritize patriarchal family structures, or devalue feminist perspectives. By endorsing these norms, women can gain social or cultural benefits within communities where hegemonic masculinity is deeply ingrained. Additionally, such participation may be a strategic choice to secure stability, safety, or power within a system that privileges men, even as it limits their autonomy.

So, we can think of hegemonic masculinity as the "top dog" of masculinity. It is the type of masculinity that society holds up as ideal. If you are seen as fitting into the hegemonic mold—assertive, tough, financially successful—you're more likely to be respected and rewarded in society. But if you don't quite fit into that mold—perhaps you are more sensitive or less interested in traditionally male pursuits such as sports—you might find yourself on the fringes, having to navigate expectations and risks that come with not aligning yourself.

Hegemonic masculinity often defines why certain types of guys seem to get more approval or power in different situations and shines a light on how those expectations shape everyone's ideas about what it means to be a masculine man. Ultimately, hegemonic masculinity theory challenges us to recognize how societal norms perpetuate inequalities and harm and limit us all, and encourages us to work towards a more inclusive and equitable society where all individuals, regardless of gender, can thrive.

Looking at infidelity through the frame of hegemonic masculinity helps reveal the emotional cost of infidelity to men. Under this framework, men are often encouraged to assert their dominance, seek multiple sexual partners, and prioritize their desires over relational fidelity. This cultural script can make infidelity seem like a demonstration of masculinity and power. Men may feel that engaging in extramarital experiences will validate their masculinity or that they will gain approval in a manner they don't feel they are getting from their primary partner. This behavior is often glamorized or excused in many cultural scripts, reinforcing the cycle of infidelity as a marker of male identity.

While societal norms might push men towards infidelity, these actions can lead to significant emotional turmoil and relationship damage. The suppression of vulnerability and emotional depth, as dictated by hegemonic masculinity, can prevent men from addressing the underlying issues in their primary relationships, making it harder to seek and maintain fulfilling connections. This can create a cycle where infidelity temporarily masks deeper dissatisfaction, only to exacerbate the problem in the long run. Thus, while hegemonic masculinity might drive men towards infidelity, it ultimately undermines their emotional well-being and relationship satisfaction.

SOCIAL EXCHANGE THEORY

Social exchange theory is a fascinating lens through which we can understand human interactions and relationships. At its core, it suggests that our social behavior is the result of an exchange process where we seek to maximize benefits and minimize costs in our interactions with others. Think of it as a sort of mental bookkeeping: we weigh the rewards we get from a relationship against the efforts and sacrifices we put into it. This theory helps explain why we choose to enter, maintain, or end relationships based on this ongoing cost-benefit analysis.

What's particularly interesting about social exchange theory is how it applies to various types of relationships, from friendships and romantic partnerships to professional and family connections. For instance, in a romantic relationship, the benefits might include love, companionship, support, and sex, while the costs could be time, emotional investment, and compromise. If the perceived rewards outweigh the costs, we are likely to stay committed even when it is challenging. However, if the costs start to overshadow the benefits we might reconsider the relationship. This dynamic isn't static; it evolves as circumstances and individual perceptions change. In other words, the longer and the deeper the relationship becomes, the greater the cost/reward ratio becomes.

Beyond personal relationships, social exchange theory also offers insights into broader social structures and organizational behavior. In workplaces, for example, employees evaluate their job satisfaction based on the rewards they receive, such as salary, recognition, and career advancement, against the demands of their role and workplace stress. Employers try to balance the benefits they provide to retain talented staff while managing operational overhead and bottom-line profits. This process at work is not unlike what we do in our romantic relationships.

When looking at men and infidelity through the lens of social exchange theory, it is perceivable that some men might weigh costs and benefits of their actions in their relationships. If the cost of staying present in the relationship is arguing and conflict, a man will likely avoid direct conflicts. Over time, these avoidance behaviors—supported by hegemonic masculinity scripts that value stoicism and avoiding emotionally vulnerable conversation—become entrenched. However, the need for connection, validation, intimacy, and more must still be met. The unspoken needs are still present even if the man doesn't know how to access them, ask for them, or create a connection with his partner that fosters them. This is where many men get lost in their own experience and will open themselves up to the opportunity for infidelity.

If a man perceives that the rewards he receives from his relationship are not greater than the costs of being in the relationship, he may intentionally or unintentionally start to consider the benefits of an extramarital relationship, such as excitement, novelty, emotional connection, conflict avoidance, or validation. If the perceived rewards, curiosity, and pleasure of an infidelity begin to outweigh the potential costs, such as getting caught (because he doesn't think he will), or emotional damage (because he has underestimated it), he might be more open to allowing the potential for an infidelity. In reality much of this decision-making is done reflexively rather than actively. It is the rare situation when someone sits down and concretely thinks about the risks and costs of infidelity as they are often caught up in the perceived benefits and excitement of getting what they think they are missing. The decision-making process is deeply influenced by how satisfied, connected, understood, and valued he feels in his current relationship and whether he feels his needs and desires are being met. Using this theoretical lens it is easier to see that—even though they are deeply painful and hurtful—infidelities are not often committed out of sinister plans but out of trying to assuage emotional needs.

Furthermore, social exchange theory helps us to understand the aftermath of infidelity. Once the infidelity is disclosed or discovered, the balance of costs and benefits shifts dramatically. The woman may reassess the relationship, considering the emotional toll, loss of trust, and potential social consequences are too high to continue. The man, on the other hand, must weigh the costs of losing his primary relationship against the benefits he perceived from his affair and the rewards he will gain from doing arduous and emotionally taxing recovery work. Having hope that the recovery work will bring rewards and benefits motivates the man to work harder during the recovery period.

FEMINIST THEORY

Feminist theory is a rich and diverse framework for understanding and addressing the inequalities and injustices that arise from gendered power dynamics in society. At its core, feminist theory seeks to analyze the ways in which gender intersects with other social categories, such as race, class, and sexuality to shape individual experiences and social structures. It challenges the traditional, patriarchal norms that are supported by hegemonic masculinity that have historically marginalized women and other gender minorities while at the same time ensuring that men are held captive by strict masculine scripts. This theory focuses on advocating for social, political, and economic equality. It is not monolithic and encompasses a variety of voices that focus on different issues, such as liberal feminism's focus on equal opportunities or radical feminism's critique of systemic patriarchy.

One of the key contributions of feminist theory is its emphasis on the lived experiences of both men and women and the importance of personal narratives in understanding broader social phenomena. By valuing these perspectives, feminist theory brings attention to issues often overlooked in the broader mainstream conversations, such as domestic violence, reproductive rights, and relationship structures. It also highlights the concept of intersectionality, coined by Kimberlé Crenshaw which explores how the intersection of a person's identities as I described them above (e.g., race, gender, class) interact to create unique modes of discrimination and privilege, offering a more nuanced and comprehensive analysis of social issues.

The root of feminist theory is not just about addressing the inequalities faced by women; it is also directly about releasing men from the restrictive gender norms and expectations that bind them. Feminist theory challenges these damaging stereotypes, advocating for a more flexible understanding of gender that allows men to embrace a fuller range of human emotions and experiences.

By promoting the idea that gender roles are socially constructed and not inherently tied to one's biological sex, feminist theory opens up new possibilities for men to engage in caregiving, emotional expression, and collaborative relationships without fear of judgment or loss of identity. These issues are critical in infidelity recovery, particularly when there is a loss of identity after disclosure or discovery. When men can experience this greater openness and equality and realize they are not solely identified by the ability to conform to toxic masculine scripts, they can better advocate for their needs in the relationship and show up for their partner and themselves more authentically. This brings greater fulfillment and healthier relationships.

Feminist theory is particularly helpful in understanding the experience for men who commit acts of infidelity. Traditional notions of masculinity emphasize dominance, sexual conquest, and emotional suppression. These ideals can create a lived experience where men feel pressured to prove their masculinity through extramarital affairs if they are not feeling fulfilled in the primary relationship and do not have the skills, insight, or perceived permission to be self-advocating outside of the masculine script. Feminist theory can help us see that infidelity can be a symptom of the unrealistic and damaging expectations placed on men by a patriarchal society.

The impact of emotional isolation in infidelity can also be explored through feminist theory. As men are socialized to avoid expressing vulnerability or seeking emotional support, they can experience deep loneliness and dissatisfaction. Men can often have a "put up and shut up" attitude, believing there is little space for them to be different based on social scripting. When their primary relationship fails to meet their emotional and identity supporting needs, some men seek connection and validation outside their marriage. One of the common needs for betrayed partners is to understand why this man had an infidelity, hoping for a concrete, specific answer. It is rare that this question can be answered so directly as the men themselves struggle to understand why they did what they did. Understanding dynamics through a feminist lens allows us to address the root causes of infidelity, promoting ways for men to express their emotions and seek support within their relationship.

HOW THE THEORIES WORK TOGETHER AND CONTRADICT EACH OTHER

When using theories to better understand our human condition, it is important to explore the benefits and pitfalls of each one. Each of the theories presented offers unique insights into gender dynamics and relationship processing—and they can support and contradict each other at the same time.

Hegemonic masculinity theory and feminist theory often align in their critique of traditional gender roles and power structures that uphold them. Hegemonic masculinity focuses on how societal norms promote a dominant form of masculinity that emphasizes power, control, and emotional suppression which can be harmful to men

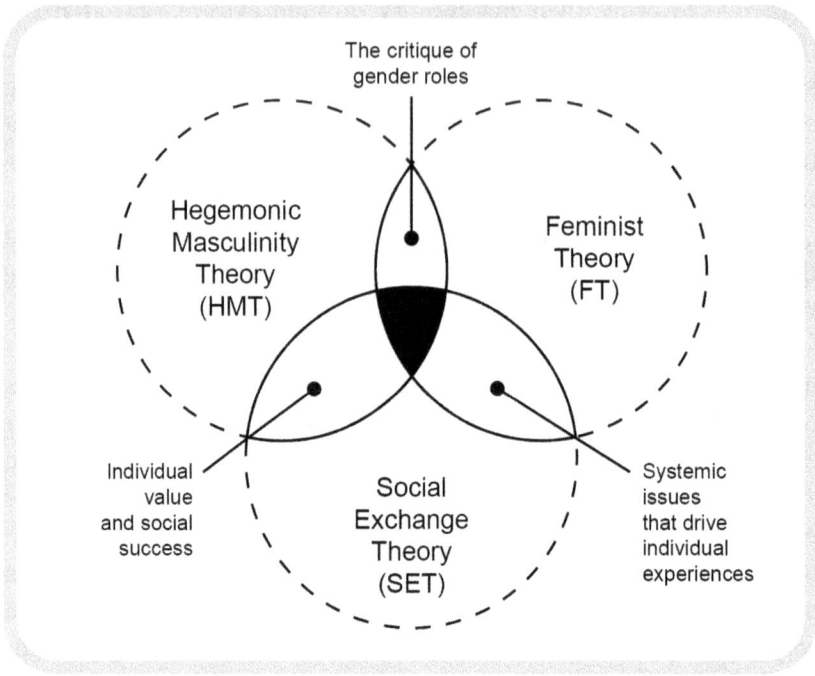

Figure 2: **The Challenge of Masculinity**

and women. Feminist theory complements this by advocating for the dismantling of these patriarchal structures. Both theories highlight the negative impact of rigid gender norms and call for a redefinition of what it means to be a man or woman in contemporary society.

These two theories also contradict each other. While hegemonic masculinity primarily focuses on the negative impacts of these norms on men and their behavior, feminist theory broadens the scope to include how these norms perpetuate gender inequality and oppress others. Feminist theory has also embraced the critical concept of inter-sectionality—the value of understanding the complex web of identities that each person has, whereas hegemonic masculinity focuses narrowly on male experiences and behaviors.

Social exchange theory can complement the other two theories by explaining how perceived rewards and costs influence our behavior within the context of the social norms. For example, a man deeply influenced by hegemonic masculinity might view infidelity as a positive that outweighs addressing the failures in his relationship that would further upset his partner, while feminist theory would critique the patriarchal values that frame such a behavior as an option.

The contradictions come in when the social exchange theory's emphasis on individual decision-making conflicts with the more societal-level analyses of the other theories. Social exchange theory often views behavior as rational and self-interested, which can overlook the deeper, systemic issues highlighted by the other lenses. For example, social exchange theory might not take into account how ingrained societal norms, power imbalances, and value structures shape what an individual might perceive as rewards and costs.

THE REAL-LIFE IMPACTS OF THE THEORIES

The theories explored here are just a small part of understanding why men operate the ways they do in society and in relationships. Human behavior is remarkably complex, shaped by a myriad of factors, including upbringing, cultural influences, personal experiences, and psychological needs. While these theories provide insight into specific behaviors like infidelity, they don't capture the full picture. Men, like everyone else, are influenced by a combination of biological drives, social expectations, emotional struggles, relationship dynamics, and individual choices. To truly understand why men act the way they do, we need to consider the broader context of their lives and the diverse influences that shape their actions.

The theories converge to illuminate how cultural norms, power dynamics, rewards and costs, and gendered socialization can suppress emotional awareness and expression in men, potentially leading to alexithymia. Alexithymia is a condition characterized by difficulty in identifying, understanding, and expressing emotions. People with alexithymia often struggle to recognize their own emotional state and may find it challenging to describe their feelings to others. This can lead to a limited emotional vocabulary and an inability to process emotions effectively. While alexithymia isn't classified as a mental disorder, it is a trait that can significantly impact interpersonal relationships and overall well-being.

In men, alexithymia can manifest in various ways. They may

come across as emotionally distant or disconnected, finding it hard to communicate their feelings or empathize with others. This can lead to misunderstandings and strained relationships, as their partners might perceive them as indifferent or uncaring. Men with alexithymia may also resort to physical activities or external solutions to cope with stress, rather than addressing the emotional roots of their issues. Understanding alexithymia can help in recognizing these behaviors and working toward better emotional communication and commitment.

The theories described here all provide valuable insights into how alexithymia can develop in men. Hegemonic masculinity theory emphasizes the predominance of traditional male traits like stoicism, self-reliance, and emotional restraint, discouraging men from expressing vulnerability or emotions. Feminist theory critiques these societal norms, highlighting how they limit men's emotional development. Social exchange theory, which views relationships as transactions, suggests that men may avoid expressing emotions if they perceive it as offering little reward or creating potential costs. Together, these theories explain how social expectations and gender norms can condition men to suppress their emotions and restrict help-seeking behaviors such as therapy or communicating openly with their partners, resulting in alexithymia.

As this socialization informs and restricts how men think, act, and feel, there are direct relationship impacts. As the bell hooks quotation indicated, men are implored to avoid behaviors that are considered feminine as they build the masculine mystique and try to live the definition of optimal masculinity. Men who hold onto such masculine ideals often believe that the discussion of personal matters is inappropriate and shameful. As such, men who are trapped in these thoughts and conceptions tend to view participation in therapy with less favor. So, when men feel emotional weakness there is often an increase in self-stigma because they have received the core messaging that men should be able to solve their own problems, develop independence, and maintain control. It is easy to see that this is not sustainable in the context of a relationship.

This core messaging can often make it very difficult for men to ask for help. This creates a sense of isolation as men might believe that asking for support is a sign of weakness or failure. They struggle internally with emotions they can't identify or express, and the idea of reaching out for assistance feels counter to the ingrained belief that they should and can handle everything on their own. This internal conflict not only exacerbates their emotional difficulties but also prevents them from finding the help they need to navigate their feelings.

Significant people in their lives, such as family, friends, and lovers, can unintentionally add to this shame and stigma. Socialization often reinforces the idea that men should be strong and self-reliant and well-meaning loved ones support the harmful notions when using phrases that are akin to "toughen up," or "be a man," even when they are not used directly to the man in question. This reinforces an expectation that help-seeking is negative and deepens men's isolation.

On the flip side, when significant others are overly supportive in pushing men to seek help, it can sometimes backfire. Men with alexithymia may already feel a sense of failure or brokenness due to their inability to express emotions and vulnerability. Overemphasis and overeagerness from loved ones to seek support can shine a spotlight on what is making the man feel inadequate or flawed. Well-intended pressure to get better or fix the issue can still reinforce that the man is not measuring up.

Navigating this delicate balance requires understanding and sensitivity. Significant others need to offer support without making the man feel judged or broken. Encouraging open dialogue about emotions in a nonconfrontational manner can help create a safe space for men to begin exploring their feelings without feeling pressured. This is most effective if done prior to any acts of infidelity: after infidelity, doing this becomes much harder.

3
▼

MASCULINE ROLE MODELS AND ROLES

Understanding how men experience relationship role models and identify what their own relationship roles should be is crucial for exploring infidelity. From a young age, as you saw in the last chapter, men are influenced by the relationships they observe, whether in their families, communities, or media. These role models shape their expectations and behaviors in relationships, impacting how they interact with partners, friends, and even themselves. These early life experiences teach young boys what relationship ideals they should have and what is expected of them in relationships when they get older. As a result, their adult patterns of relationship behavior are then replayed and recrafted with their partners—for better or worse. This understanding can help us support men in developing authentic, fulfilling relationships and breaking free from restrictive social norms that hinder their emotional development. Post-infidelity, having these understandings can help us to better understand how such hurtful decisions and behaviors happened.

THE POWER OF ROLE MODELS

From a social exchange theory framework, relationship activities, discussions, and power dynamics are grounded in a cost/reward system that produces a sense of reciprocity and accountability (Sprecher). How young men see reciprocity and accountability modeled informs what they should expect from their partner and what level of personal responsibility is being sought from them. As relationships develop and become more long-term, they increase in complexity, decreasing in novelty, so that the cost/reward equation begins to shift.

Relationships that were fun, easy, and active in the beginning can begin to feel like work and become tedious as time goes on. It is the early life experiences of how relationships were modeled that is a significant influence on how men handle these shifts in developing relationships.

Through a national study I have conducted and my years of clinical work with men and infidelity, I have found that when asked about their relationship role models, men often describe two significant extremes. On one hand, many men recount role models whose relationships appeared conflict-free and idealistic. These relationships seemed perfect on the surface but did not provide any real lessons in intimacy or conflict resolution because conflicts were never openly displayed or addressed. This left these men without tools to navigate the inevitable disagreements and emotional challenges that would arise in their own relationships.

In my 2020 national study on men and infidelity, I was careful to include questions about the early relationship role models the men had experienced. Here are some quotations from what those with an idealistic, low-conflict model shared:

> *What I saw on TV. My idea of a marriage or a husband and wife were what I saw on TV, or the Disney movies, or the Cleavers, Dick Van Dyke and Mary Tyler Moore, and you know, everything was really perfect. (Daniel)*

> *My parents and grandparents, you know, had always been together, right?!? There was no divorce ... um nothing like that. (Isaac)*

Being grown up with the man ... that man. The provider. It was what was expected. (George)

On the other end of the spectrum, some men in my study grew up in chaotic and openly dysfunctional homes, observing role models who were hurtful to each other, engaged in infidelity, and showed little to no emotional connection. These relationships often ended in break-ups, leaving a lasting impression of instability and distrust. Men who witnessed this dynamic frequently internalized the negative patterns, believing that relationships were inherently tumultuous and fraught with betrayal. These experiences and the resulting beliefs can make it difficult for them to build healthy, trusting adult relationships of their own, as they lack positive examples to emulate. Here is some of what those men said:

I don't remember them being very warm. (Nate)

I am a child of divorce. I am a grandchild of divorce. My dad always stepped out on my mom. My grandfather stepped out on my grandmother. (Brian)

They were emotionally bankrupt. They probably shouldn't have had kids. (Evan)

My mom and dad divorced when I was one. They were always at each other's throats ... mom got cancer and her boyfriend was abusive. (Harry)

My father taught me that a partner should be strong, domineering, and controlling. (John)

Both extremes—conflict-free but emotionally distant relationships and conflict-ridden, unstable ones—highlight a crucial gap in the relationship skills they are passed down. Men who only see idealized relationships don't learn how to advocate for themselves, communicate in times of challenge, and handle conflict constructively, while those who only see destructive patterns may struggle to believe in or build healthy connections. Recognizing these patterns is the first step toward addressing them, helping men to develop the skills necessary for intimate, resilient, and fulfilling relationships.

Some men in the study had confusing role models. This is challenging because these men tend to move forward in relationships in a less explicitly intentional manner. For example:

My dad got married when he was 22; my brother got married when he was 22. I thought that is what I should do and I did it. (Frank)

I would just see how everyone else was acting and then I would go, "Okay, that's what I need to do." (Evan)

In asking the men in my study who had committed infidelity about their relationship role models growing up, what was especially interesting was how they tensed and shrugged when asked, "Who were your relationship role models and what did you learn from them?" It showed me that the men had not been aware of the lessons of their earlier life and the impacts of those lessons they had experienced. It was only after getting caught in infidelity that they began this type of reflection. They had never considered the unspoken teachings and set of expectations they had been subtly given on how to be in a boyfriend-girlfriend or husband-wife relationship, or considered that how they behaved once in that relationship had any direct correlation back to what they had experienced as boys.

When asked about such role models and what they had learned about relationships as they were growing up, every participant in the study took a long pause before answering. Several men alluded to the fact that they had never even considered the question before. Many, after taking that moment of pause, were quick to counter that their relationship role models were not their parents, unless negative role modeling was to be considered. Men used words like "embarrassment," "shame," "absent," "disconnect," and "unfaithful" to name messages received from parental role models. Countering this experience, other men, regardless of whether they considered their parents to be clear role models, used words like "loving," "affectionate," "doting," and "traditional."

Not one participant in my study on infidelity named their parents as a clear role model of how they believed they should be in their own relationship. Aligning with hegemonic masculinity theory, many men described that *absolutely no one* taught them how to be a good partner, but they identified with sentiments such as:

I'm the dude.... I did most of the gender roles. (Nate)

The next logical thing is, you know, solidify the relationship, get married to do all of the other things. (Charles)

Most participants agreed that their relationship education was not provided, and they had to make assumptions based on their surroundings and peers regarding how they were expected to present themselves. The men talked about how they looked to the environments for guidance, making statements such as "I don't know ... something about growing up in this city, and very tuned into what other people were doing, the cars they were driving, the vacations they were taking." (Daniel)

Brian shared, "A lot of my friends' parents were divorced or based on what I saw of their parents, they should have been divorced. I knew that my, I always suspected, kind of knew, my dad stepped out on my mom. Um, and knew my grandfather and grandmother on my mother's side cheated on each other."

Intergenerational modeling was common as some men looked to grandparents and other extended family members. Oscar, describing his grandparents, shared, "They've been together for 50 years ... selfless for each other, they similarly had a very traditional kind of set up between husband and wife." When discussing intergenerational influences, men stated family culture as well as the direct modeling they received. "I come from a Catholic family and all that comes with it" (Luke).

Understanding these patterns is critical when infidelity is discovered, as it can significantly aid in the recovery process. Recognizing the influence of relationship role models helps both partners understand the underlying dynamics that may have contributed to the infidelity. For men who grew up with conflict-free but emotionally distant role models, it becomes essential to learn how to engage in healthy conflict resolution and build genuine intimacy. This awareness can guide them in developing the emotional skills they need to rebuild trust and communicate more effectively with their partner.

For those who observed hurtful, unstable relationships, understanding these patterns can help break the cycle of negative behavior. It allows them to see how past experiences have shaped their expectations and actions in their own relationships. This awareness can be the first step toward creating new, healthier patterns of interaction.

By addressing these deep-seated influences, men can work towards developing a more secure and stable relationship dynamic, fostering a more supportive environment for both partners to heal.

Ultimately, exploring these relationship role models provides a roadmap for recovery. It offers insight into some of the root causes of infidelity and highlights areas where growth and change are needed. By addressing these foundational issues, men and their partners can work together to rebuild trust, improve communication, and create openness. This process not only aids in healing from the immediate pain of infidelity but also sets the stage for a more connected and fulfilling partnership in the future.

UNDERSTANDING RELATIONSHIP "JOBS"

Relationship jobs are the responsibilities that individuals take on within their partnerships. These "jobs" can be diverse and expansive depending on the context of the partnership. Each person brings their own expectations, preferences, and skills to these roles based on their upbringing, cultural norms, personal experiences in life, and previous relationships. Understanding what your relationship job is and what your partner perceives theirs to be is essential for fostering a balanced and harmonious connection.

Relationship jobs can significantly define how we connect with one another. For instance, if one partner sees their job as being an emotional supporter, they may focus on providing comfort and understanding, while expecting the same in return. Conversely, if one partner takes on the job of problem-solver, they may approach issues with a solution-oriented mindset, potentially overlooking the emotional aspects that need addressing. Recognizing and discussing these roles can help partners better align their efforts and expectations, ensuring that both emotional and practical needs are met.

Being aware of our relationship jobs can help us avoid misunderstandings and conflicts. When roles are clearly defined and mutually agreed upon, it creates a sense of teamwork and shared responsibility. However, if these roles are assumed without discussion, it can lead to feelings of imbalance or resentment. By openly communicating about what each partner's relationship job entails, couples can work together more effectively, supporting each other in ways that feel meaningful and fulfilling. This mutual understanding and cooperation lay the foundation for a stronger, more connected relationship.

It is not uncommon for men not to consider and be unaware of what their relationship jobs are. Men are not often raised or taught to be curious about their relationship jobs, instead making assumptions based on societal messages rooted in hegemonic masculinity. From a young age, many men are conditioned to adopt traditional roles without questioning them—such as being a provider or fixer and problem-solver. These roles are often reinforced by cultural norms, media portrayals, and family expectations, leaving little room for exploration or discussion about other potential responsibilities that could be beneficial within a relationship. Focusing on fulfilling these traditional roles, many men assume this is the sole way to show their value and commitment. This lack of curiosity can lead to an overly narrow view of how they can contribute to and connect within their partnerships.

The result of these assumptions can lead to imbalances and unmet emotional needs for both partners. It is important to encourage men to be more inquisitive about their relationship jobs and think outside the box in order to break down rigid and unfulfilling expectations that lead to discontent.

In my national study, I asked my male respondents what they believed their relationship jobs to be. Most of the men I surveyed struggled with the question. Many found it challenging to articulate their specific roles within their relationships, often because they had never given it much thought or felt uncertain about their contributions beyond the traditional expectations of providing and protecting. This difficulty highlights a broader issue: many men have not been encouraged to deeply consider or discuss the various aspects of their relationship roles. As a result, they may lack clarity on how to engage more fully and equitably with their partners, which is crucial for rebuilding trust and fostering a healthier, more balanced dynamic after infidelity.

In the study, men overwhelmingly identified only four core job roles: provider, fixer, stabilizer, and desired sex partner. This narrow focus reflects the traditional expectations placed on men and highlights the limited scope of how they view their own contributions to a relationship. As providers, they felt responsible for the financial well-being of their family, ensuring the material needs were met. As fixers, they took on the role of problem-solving and handling crises, often prioritizing practical solutions over emotional support. As stabilizers, they aimed to maintain peace and order, often by suppressing their own emotions and actively avoiding direct conflict—which often resulted in direct conflict. Lastly, as desired sex partner, they felt the pressure to meet social and relational sexual expectations and validate their worth through sexual performance. These men reported that if sexual connection was not good with their partner, it indicated they were failing in their roles as provider, fixer, and stabilizer. They felt that a lack of sexual satisfaction was a direct reflection of their overall performance and worth in the relationship.

In the study, when men were asked what they thought their relationship jobs were, responses were telling:

"Being grown up, the man. The provider." (George)

"You provide for a stable lifestyle." (Oscar)

"You make every effort to fix it." (Evan)

TO PROVIDE

Men often feel immense pressure to be good providers, a responsibility deeply rooted in traditional gender roles and societal expectations. From a young age, many men are taught that their worth is closely tied to their ability to provide financially and ensure the well-being of their family. This message is often unintentionally reinforced by women when they express admiration and gratitude for a man with resources, which, while well-meaning, can underscore the expectation that this is a core function of men. The result is added pressure to perform. During times of financial stress, women might unintentionally lean more on their male partners for stability, especially when systems of power still underpay women for their work. These greater systems of power that privilege male earning over female earning carry unexplored messages of pressure on men to provide. This pressure can create a significant burden as men strive to meet these expectations, often at the expense of their own emotional health and personal fulfillment. The fear of failing in this role can be overwhelming, leading to stress and anxiety, and making it difficult to balance other important aspects of a relationship.

The men in the study identified this need to provide as their primary role in the relationship. A curious fact in their responses was that the concept of being a provider was not focused on the partnership solely but on the greater family and household dynamic. Every man in the study identified that the ability to ensure he was bringing in enough resources was paramount. Providing was discussed in terms of financial security, appropriate housing, transportation, vacation/entertainment, and social identity through work. The men talked about not providing enough being the primary reason for disconnect in their relationship. They discussed holding the belief their partners valued their ability to provide as core to their own perceived value as a partner.

Comments such as "make a lot of money," "provide materially and everything else will take care of itself," and "be the breadwinner" reinforced how the men felt their value in the relationship was understood. One clear comment from a participant summed it up powerfully: "I relied too much on my parents for their help instead of standing on my own feet ... living up to my potential ... my wife was disappointed; she thought she married better." (Daniel) Providing security was also deeply impactful to the men. One respondent stated clearly that his social obligation was "to make sure your wife and kids are taken care of" (Brian), and his success as a man was determined by this ability.

The way the men in the study talked about the role of the provider speaks directly to how they manage the cost/benefit analysis of their relationship in their own heads. When the men talked about living up to their potential or ensuring their family is secure and taken care of, it was perceived to be their primary job above all others.

TO STABILIZE

Secondarily to being a provider, the men in my study talked about the importance of stabilizing the relationship and family. A core message of masculinity men are taught is to maintain calm and order, to be the rock during turbulent times, and to provide a sense of stability for their partners and families. These messages are reinforced by social messages that equate masculinity with emotional restraint and problem-solving ability. When men expect to be the steadying force, it can create significant stress as they may feel they must suppress their own emotional needs and anxieties to meet these expectations. This pressure to be perpetually composed and supportive, even when they are struggling internally, can lead to emotional strain and difficulties in addressing their own needs within the relationship.

When asked what stabilizing meant, the men in the study universally described activities that were outward-facing but not addressing their own needs. If children were involved, men wanted to be good co-parents even if they didn't know what that entailed. Many men used phrases such as "keep Mom from getting upset" and "just keep everyone happy."

What was constant for these men was their belief that being a stabilizer was a role of sheer strength as they had to be on constant guard for the next eruption of emotion. As discussed earlier, unexpected or unpredictable emotional responses can be dysregulating for men, as a core understanding that men remain stoic. This belief that bottling up the stress while shouldering the emotional load of others is the basic expectation. This social pressure was true even for the most progressive men in the study: "I was a caretaker. I view myself as a feminist, so I don't like the macho feel on that ... [laughs] the fallacy of equity in relationship" (Luke). Yet, when asked why he did not talk to his wife about his emotional challenges, he said that his role as caretaker was to take care of her, not to be taken care of. So, even a progressive man who believes he is challenging hegemonic patriarchy was still profoundly impacted by the deep roots of the social norms he grew up with.

The attempt at being a good stabilizer often has men relying on the stoic strength they believe they must lead with. This strength is focused on creating consistency out of chaos, often by trying to reduce the emotionality of others—and this is experienced more as a burden than pride. Having the need to hold onto a sense of masculinity and identity, many men struggled with nurturance and their understanding of it as a more feminine approach. Some of the men in the study were able to sense they earned additional respect by doing a job that was less gender-conforming. When that respect was articulated and expressed, the men were more able to hold it. When the respect did not come openly, the men reported feeling disrespected and disregarded.

One study participant shared his disillusionment at not getting his investment to yield positive returns: "My wife transitioned to a new job and it was a big move for her.... It was a big-time commitment for her ... she was really absorbed in her job.... I kept my work at work so I could have that time at home with my kids and partner … and I remember feeling resentful that it wasn't happening for her, and I also remember feeling mad that her organization prides itself on work/life balance, and it's always like fucking bullshit because you don't take any." (Luke) When men in the study tried to lean into the stabilizer and provider roles and began to feel invisible or taken for granted, resentment would grow.

To Fix

Once the primary functions of providing and stabilizing were managed, the men quickly identified the job of being a fixer. Young boys are taught that their value lies in their ability to solve problems. This expectation is then reinforced in a multitude of ways as they mature. Portrayals of successful men in media, books, movies, and society in general depict men as the go-to guy who is practical, stoic, and clear-headed. When faced with personal or relationship issues, men might feel compelled to act quickly to fix things rather than address underlying emotional concerns. This drive to fix can increase stress and frustration especially when solutions are not straightforward or when they feel their efforts are unseen or underappreciated. This often means that men are missing the critical function of emotional connection in favor of quick solutions.

In the simplest terms, the fixer was described as the person who did male gender-conforming functions such as taking out the trash, tending to the car, doing the landscaping, and other activities that are modes of support and define hegemonic masculinity between men and women.

While the fixer role was not seen as critical as the provider and stabilizer roles, the fixer identity was present for all men in the study. All the men in the study deemed being successful in this gender performativity: they did not want to be seen as not manly enough. They discussed that doing mundane tasks confirmed their identity and investment in the relationship. Whether it was to be a cleaner-upper, disciplinarian for the children or pets, or simply being the "go-to guy," this function represented a core identity facet across all respondents in the study.

This need to fix and be acknowledged for it can be understood as part of the internal battles men experience as they try to solidify their role within the partnership and family. What it means to be a good partner and father in contemporary society is shifting quickly. However men can still struggle and operate from more traditional social messaging that feels inconsistent and confusing when they diverge from strict gender roles.

One of the curious outcomes of this study was that men struggled to identify what they needed fixed for themselves. Because fixing was such an outward focus and activity, a reciprocal function was not considered. As Alan stated, "For my own needs? That was my stuff, not hers." And George said, "I wish I could talk about issues and stuff more with her and feelings, and you know, needs and wants. I still have this fear of 'I don't deserve it' or 'I'm going to get rejected.'" Oscar noted that he resorted to negative masculine traits when he was challenged to address his own needs or failings. He shared that he struggled to do a good job at communicating needs "and just generally being effective in communication in our relationship…. My general mentality was to be very aggressive to resolve things immediately … to bring things at the forefront and you know, I think that would often come in the form of picking fights or being very direct in a way that could hurt her feelings."

Some of the men discussed trying to share their needs with their partners, but if those attempts weren't met with immediate openness and caring, they quickly stopped their efforts and resorted to turning inward. Once an attempt is made unsuccessfully, a common theme was that the men would not try again. This would be consistent with the negative stoic values that would diminish vulnerability of the men and close doors in the relationship.

To Be a Desired Sex Partner

The final job role the men described was discussed not by answering my core question about what they thought their relationship job was, but in describing how they experienced failure and relational breakdown while attempting the first three roles they thought were expected of them. From a social exchange perspective, we can understand that the men saw that being a desired sex partner was a reward, benefit, and confirmation of their successfully completing the provider, stabilizer, and fixer functions.

Because sex is never experienced in a vacuum, but rather exists through complex and powerful relationship dynamics, understanding how the men made such connections within their relationship to their jobs and perceived value is informative. First, the men defined sex broadly. With a primary value on penetrative sex, other activities such as oral sex, fondling, massage, and various foreplay also had deep value. Men in the study could identify significant shifts in their sexual connections for a variety of reasons, such as birth of a child, libidos that emerged as unbalanced over time, exhaustion from managing an increasingly complex home and life, life goals misaligned with their partner's, previous sexual trauma, and emotional discord in the relationship.

Many men grow up assuming that having children is just part of their role in marriage—that reproduction is a natural and expected outcome of their sexual relationship. The idea of infertility often doesn't cross their minds, as the cultural narrative tends to portray men as perpetually fertile and focused more on virility than vulnerability. It's only when faced with the reality of fertility struggles, either their own or their partner's, that they begin to question these assumptions. This can be a deeply unsettling experience, challenging their sense of identity, purpose, and even their worth in the relationship.

This area of exploration within the study had the most complicated language of all. It became clear early on that the men struggled to talk about their sex life with their partner, their partner's needs, and sex in general. When talking about sex with an affair partner, the men were more open and casual than when talking about their sexual connection with their relationship partners. There is a notion that sex should be spontaneous and not talked about and this manner of sexual connection was more available with affair partners than with relationship partners. Because sex with relationship partners becomes rooted in a far more complex relationship than with affair partners, structure and routine are increased while spontaneity and a lack of planning in sex are diminished.

Nate described compartmentalizing during his extramarital affair, which made the affair easier to process. He shared, "I never believed in compartmentalization and blah blah blah, but I was. It certainly happens." Michael shared that when sex was becoming problematic, he couldn't talk to his wife and he turned inward to avoid the conflict. He said, "Sex wasn't there. I think it had been declining for some time and

I think I slipped into substituting that originally with pornography. And, for me, that was a slippery slope. In the end what that transpired to was finding these hookup sites where they had pictures. Some of the pictures, for example the more intimate pictures, were locked. You're chatting with these people and they unlock them for you." Michael reported that his wife had just given birth, and they were fighting mostly about sex from his perspective, but on deeper reflection he identified that it was probably more about attention than sex. Sex was just the confirmation of attention.

Understanding the Roles

These roles, while important, do not encompass the full range of what a healthy, balanced relationship requires. The emphasis on these four areas can lead to neglect of other crucial aspects, such as emotional intimacy, effective communication, keeping one's own physical and emotional health, negotiating and holding important boundaries, personal evolution, being intentional, showing curiosity, and more. By focusing on traditional roles, men may miss opportunities to connect with partners on a deeper level and to share the emotional labor that is essential for a thriving relationship. My study underscores the need for broader discussion about relationship roles, encouraging men to explore and embrace a more diverse array of engagements that contribute to a more fulfilling and equitable partnership, ultimately making men feel more appreciated and valued as they get more meaningful responses from their partners.

Exploring Relationship Jobs

Social and cultural norms make it deeply challenging for both men and their female partners to explore and talk about relationship jobs. While women often want men to be emotionally vulnerable and open, and to take on more varied relationship jobs, they can sometimes unconsciously send mixed messages. On one hand, they may demand more emotional availability and participation, expect the man to go to therapy, and participate differently in family and household duties. On the other hand, societal expectations and ingrained habits can cause women to misunderstand why men are resistant to changes, and sometimes even cause women to reinforce traditional gender roles during moments of stress or conflict. An example is when women expect their male partners to be emotionally strong and grounded and react in a confused manner when men struggle with this. This can confuse men, making them feel unsure about how to navigate their experiences and roles and how to meet their partner's needs and expectations at the same time. The key is for both partners to recognize these mixed messages and work together to create a clear, supportive path toward more balanced and fulfilling relationship dynamics.

These conversations are challenging in the best of times. They require a deep insight, self-reflection, and vulnerability. Having these important conversations about relationship jobs after infidelity are fraught with danger, fear, and triggers once trust has been broken and neither partner feels secure. Infidelity shakes the very foundation of a relationship, making it difficult to engage in vulnerable and honest discussions.

While both partners are dealing with the intense emotions, fears, and hurts of infidelity, they are not dealing with the same injuries—which can cloud their thinking and processing. For the betrayed partner, the fear of being hurt again and believing that the relationship and commitment were a lie can make trusting and opening up terrifying while experiencing these intense emotions. For the partner who committed infidelity, struggling with guilt, shame, and defensiveness while fearing additional blame and criticism can make these conversations impossible.

In this delicate situation, discussing relationship jobs can feel overwhelming and an unattainable goal. The betrayed partner might question whether the cheater truly wants to and can genuinely fulfill their roles going forward, and whether they can rely on them for emotional and practical support. The partner who cheated might feel immense pressure to prove their commitment and reliability while also grappling with their own insecurities and uncertainties. This can often lead the man to agree to anything just to "provide, fix, and stabilize" the conflict as they retreat to old narratives and understandings. The lack of trust and the increasing emotional volatility make it feel impossible to have constructive conversations about how to rebalance responsibilities and rebuild the relationship.

Despite these challenges, it is crucial for couples to address these issues to move forward. Establishing new patterns and clearer expectations can help rebuild trust and create a more stable foundation. Both partners need to approach these conversations with patience, empathy, and a willingness to listen and understand each other's pain and perspectives. Because these conversations require new skills and approaches, it is highly recommended that a trained therapist with a specialty in infidelity recovery is brought into balance and helps both partners grow and heal.

Clinicians walk a tenuous tightrope when first starting to work with new clients who have experienced infidelity. Not only is trust broken between the partners, but trust must also be created with the clinician—especially if it is not a preexisting therapeutic relationship. When I start working with a new couple in the wake of infidelity, I am quite clear that the person who committed the act of infidelity is not my client. The person who was betrayed is also not my client. My client is the relationship between them. It is important to make this distinction because it alleviates the natural tendency for partners to want to have the therapist be on their side, to defend them and keep them safe. Infidelity recovery requires that both partners are put in a dynamic where both can be safe and vulnerable knowing the therapist will help to navigate the challenges they are trying to resolve.

I often think in pictures and use analogies to explain my thinking and the process we are going through. The first analogy that couples get early in the process is what I call the Boulder on the Beach. It goes like this:

> You and your beloved live on a little private beach and you love living on the beach. You think life on the beach is pretty great. Then, one night while you are sleeping, a giant boulder drops in the center of your beach. You wake up and are shocked and dismayed that your beautiful beach is ruined. Your view is ruined. You can't maneuver around the beach anymore. Your entire existence on the beach feels ruined. You now have a few choices. You can leave the beach and try to start a new life elsewhere. You can wait for time and tide to break down or move the boulder—and it will, but you will be long gone by the time that happens. Or you and your partner can start banging on the boulder hoping to get parts of it to chip off. Maybe you get a crack started in the boulder. Eventually the boulder will split. You continue to work together to break the boulder. It is exhausting and slow work, but eventually you end up with some significant rocks. Maybe you use the rocks to create an

edge on your beach or you keep breaking the rocks until they become gravel and part of the sand of your beach. The choices are yours. No choice is an easy one and no choice makes the transition quick. Any choice you make requires both of you to labor and invest in something. What will it be?

I want the couple to move the problems out from the space between them and into the space across the room. Only when we can look at the problems together rather than feeling it is the impassible chasm between us can we have movement. Much like the boulder, we must work together with the common goal. Sometimes we bang the boulder side by side, sometimes we bang the boulder from opposite sides … but we are banging the boulder and not attacking each other. It is a unified process, which in times of uncertainty can bring an important albeit tenuous sense of connectedness.

This analogy often leads to the question: so what does that work look like? How will we do this work? How do we work with you in therapy? This leads to the second analogy—that of the recording studio. I tell the couple that our work together is like being in a recording studio. They are the artists with the big headphones and dish mic and lots of foam eggcrate around them. They are going to sing their song. I am the sound engineer behind the glass. I have all the slide levers that I am going to slide up and down, moving from left to right and back again. Some levers are about sex, some about their childhood, some about parenting, some about money, some about work, some about communication, and so on.

My job is to bring in all of the factors and modulate them so they can all be integrated together to help them get just the right tone. We will spend some time on one area and then move to another, eventually coming back as we move across the levers. We move across the levers because if we stay in one area too long, we can be quite triggered and lose context of the rest of the relationship. We will address all the issues, but we have to do it in context of the whole relationship, or we lose the perspective of what we are trying to accomplish.

Once partners can see there is a space where they can work, even if they are deeply hurt, scared, or unbelieving that change can happen, the deconstruction of the infidelity can begin to happen.

4
▼

DISENFRANCHISED GRIEF: THE SILENT CHALLENGE

Disenfranchised grief, by its very definition, is an experience that cannot be spoken and shared. When grief remains unexpressed, its connection to infidelity by both partners is deeply misunderstood and one of the greatest challenges to overcome in recovery. Both the betrayed partner and the one who strayed can experience this painful dynamic. The betrayed partner might struggle with the pain of their loss and injury but also feel silenced when they feel they can't discuss the deep pain with others or feel silenced when they do, told to simply leave the relationship without consideration.

Meanwhile the betrayer can be overwhelmed by their own sense of shame and guilt, finding it difficult to express their grief over what they've lost—the relationship they hoped for, trust, and even a sense of self. Because this grief is not expressed, it can isolate both partners, making the road to healing even more complex.

For men who have betrayed their partner, talking openly about their wrongdoings is an immense struggle, largely due to the pressures of hegemonic masculinity. This social expectation pushes men to appear strong, confident, in control, and emotionally invulnerable.

Admitting to infidelity means acknowledging that they've failed—not only as a partner, but also as a man who is supposed to uphold certain ideals. By owning up to their actions, they confront the reality that they've fallen short of the standards set by themselves, their partner, and the people around them.

This admission can feel like a direct attack on their identity, which is often closely tied to being competent and dependable. It's not just about confessing a mistake; it's about facing the reality that they've let down those they care about most, and in their eyes, diminished their own worth. For many men, that fear of judgment—both internal and external—creates a significant barrier to fully owning their actions and starting the process of healing.

This struggle is further complicated by the betrayed partner's reactions. It is important for his partner to be authentic in her expression of pain and communicate her experience as a result of the betrayal. Betrayal is never a singular issue. It so often triggers previous hurts or traumas from earlier relationships, self-doubt, anxiety, or other concerns being managed by the betrayed partner. The resulting expressions of shock, pain, and dismay can be a wide spectrum of reactions that are quickly moving, shifting, and unpredictable. All of this is to be expected. It is important for the man to experience this with her, develop the capacity to be in the moment with her, and to communicate his desire to repair the relationship. Based on how those expressions of pain are communicated can cause additional challenges for the man that he must find a path to managing.

When a woman expresses her pain and hurt with intensity—whether through anger, sadness, or deep resentment—it can overwhelm the man, triggering his defense mechanisms. He may feel attacked or cornered, leading him to react defensively or shut down emotionally. In these moments, instead of focusing on her pain, he becomes fixated on his own need to protect what remains of his dignity. Defensiveness becomes a shield to avoid the shame and guilt that surface when he faces the full weight of her emotions. This reaction often halts any meaningful communication and creates more distance between them, making recovery even more difficult.

At the same time, many men fall into a well of helplessness when faced with their partner's intense emotions. Seeing the magnitude of her pain can leave him feeling completely unequipped to respond in a way that will ease her suffering. The more she expresses how deeply wounded she is, the more he might believe that no action he takes can ever repair the damage. He's stuck in a place where he wants to make things better but feels paralyzed, unsure of how to navigate her emotions or address the hurt he has caused. This helplessness can lead him to withdraw or disengage, further feeding her sense of abandonment, and deepening the emotional divide.

When the betrayed partner minimizes her pain or doesn't openly express it, the situation becomes even more complex. In these cases, the man might mistakenly assume that the lack of visible emotion means he doesn't need to address the damage he's caused. He may interpret her silence or emotional restraint as a sign that she's moved on or that the infidelity wasn't as hurtful as it seemed. This leads to compartmentalization, where he mentally boxes up the issue, believing that as long as it is not actively discussed, it doesn't need to be dealt with. This mindset allows the wound to fester beneath the surface, where resentment and unresolved hurt can quietly grow over time.

The danger in this dynamic is that unspoken pain doesn't disappear; it lingers and influences the relationship in subtle but powerful ways. Without addressing the underlying emotional injury, the man avoids truly taking responsibility for the betrayal, leaving his partner to carry the weight of her unresolved feelings alone. Over time, this can lead to an erosion of trust and intimacy, as the partner's pain, though hidden, manifests in other forms—like emotional distance, passive aggressiveness, or a growing sense of disconnection in many forms. By not acknowledging and addressing the impact of the infidelity, the couple risks building a fragile foundation for their future, one that's prone to crumbling under the pressure of unspoken hurts.

Disenfranchised grief often shows up for men in therapy after infidelity is discovered in subtle but powerful ways. These men are not only dealing with the loss of trust and stability in their relationships, but they also grapple with unacknowledged grief about the life they thought they would have. Their pain is complicated because they often feel unworthy of sympathy or support, given that they are the ones who caused the betrayal. The societal narrative tends to position men as emotionally detached or less affected by relationship issues, making it harder for them to process and express their grief openly.

In therapy, this disenfranchised grief can manifest as intense shame or defensiveness. Men may struggle to articulate the loss they feel because they don't believe they deserve to grieve, especially when the focus tends to be on the hurt partner's suffering. Their grief, though real, lacks validation from others, and often from themselves. This emotional isolation exacerbates feelings of guilt and hinders the healing process, as they are grieving not only the damage done to their relationship but also their sense of identity as a trustworthy partner or a good person.

The complexity of disenfranchised grief deepens when men's partners expect them to show regret and sorrow while taking full ownership of their actions. These expectations, though valid, can create a difficult emotional conflict for the men. On one hand, they are trying to demonstrate accountability, remorse, and empathy for the hurt they've caused. On the other hand, they are privately mourning the losses that infidelity has brought to their own lives—such as the collapse of their self-image, security, public scrutiny, embarrassment, or even aspects of their relationship that were important to them. The need to focus entirely on their partner's healing can leave them feeling unseen in their own emotional struggles, further burying their grief.

This dynamic often results in men feeling trapped between the need to show visible regret and the suppression of their own complex emotions. In therapy, men might voice that while they do feel genuine sorrow for the harm they've caused, there's also a sense of personal loss that they don't know how to reconcile. Without space to explore their grief, they may become emotionally withdrawn or overly focused on justifying their behavior to protect against further emotional pain. The unspoken grief over losing their partner's love, respect, or the life they once shared creates internal conflict that can undermine their attempts at genuine ownership and repair.

Furthermore, when men don't have the chance to process their grief, their partners may misinterpret their emotional distance as a lack of remorse or commitment to making things right. This can lead to a damaging cycle where the partner feels that their pain is not fully recognized, and the betraying partner feels even more alienated from their own emotional experience. Therapy can be essential in breaking this cycle by allowing both partners to see the full spectrum of emotions at play—validating the betrayed partner's pain while also creating space for the betrayer to process their disenfranchised grief. This holistic approach can foster deeper understanding and more authentic repair in the relationship.

Another challenge to processing disenfranchised grief is when men lack strong social connections or friends to turn to outside of therapy so their experience of disenfranchised grief becomes even more isolating. Men often develop friendships that, while close and meaningful, tend to lack the practice of openly discussing deep emotional feelings. These relationships may focus on shared activities or experiences—like sports, hobbies, or work—but rarely venture into vulnerable emotional terrain. Culturally, men are often socialized to value strength, independence, and stoicism, which can make it difficult for them to bring up sensitive topics like grief, shame, or regret. As a result, when they face a crisis such as infidelity, they find that these friendships, though supportive in other ways, don't provide the emotional depth needed for genuine processing.

This lack of emotional openness means that when men need to express feelings of guilt, sorrow, or confusion, they may not have the tools—or the right environment—to do so. They might fear being judged, seen as weak, or even alienating their friends by discussing personal struggles in a way that feels unfamiliar within the friendship dynamic. Consequently, they often keep these emotions bottled up, which reinforces their sense of isolation. When emotional processing and support are needed the most, it simply isn't available, leaving men to navigate complex feelings largely on their own or in therapy, further straining their emotional well-being.

Infidelity already brings a heavy emotional burden, and without trusted confidants to process their feelings, these men often feel trapped. Friends are typically a source of unconditional support during crises, but for men who've been unfaithful, there may be a reluctance to share due to fear of judgment or rejection. This lack of an emotional outlet outside of therapy compounds their sense of isolation and reinforces the feeling that they have to carry their grief alone, deepening the sense of disenfranchisement.

When the betrayed partner and the therapist are the only people they feel they can talk to, the pressure to manage their emotions in a certain way intensifies. In the presence of their partner, men may feel they need to constantly demonstrate remorse and focus exclusively on the partner's healing, making it hard to explore their own grief without seeming selfish or dismissive of the partner's pain. In therapy, they might feel somewhat more comfortable, but even then, the therapist is often seen as someone who is helping facilitate the repair of the relationship, which can make the man feel that even in this space, his personal grief isn't fully validated. This dynamic can prevent him from truly letting his guard down and acknowledging the full depth of his own emotional experience.

The absence of external social support can leave men feeling emotionally exhausted, as they feel they must always be "on"—always focused on fixing the relationship, showing regret, or taking responsibility. Without the relief of venting or processing in a non-judgmental environment, they may begin to feel emotionally disconnected or even resentful, further complicating the healing process. Therapy becomes a crucial space for these men to unpack these layered emotions, but when it's the only outlet, it can sometimes feel inadequate, leaving them with unresolved grief that may slow or derail their recovery. Expanding their social support network or helping them build connections becomes key in allowing them to work through their grief more fully and authentically.

Disenfranchised grief becomes even more pronounced when the exposure of infidelity extends beyond the couple and into their larger social circle, particularly when children, family members, or friends become aware of the betrayal. When others—especially those closest to them—witness the pain of the betrayed partner firsthand, the man often becomes the focal point of blame and judgment. In these moments, his own emotional experience is further marginalized, as the collective concern typically centers on the suffering of the betrayed partner. The public nature of this exposure leaves little room for him to process his feelings of loss, shame, or grief, as he is primarily seen through the lens of his actions and their consequences.

This public scrutiny makes it nearly impossible for the man to access a safe space where he can reflect on his own emotions without facing criticism. As everyone rallies around the betrayed partner, offering support and validating their pain, the man's experience is invalidated, critiqued, and judged, reinforcing his disenfranchised grief. He may feel as though he has no right to mourn what has been lost—whether it's the relationship as it once was, his role as a father or partner, or his own self-image—because the overwhelming narrative is focused on the betrayed partner's suffering. This absence of emotional refuge amplifies his isolation and can hinder his ability to genuinely engage in the healing process, as there is no space for his grief to be acknowledged or processed in a way that allows for growth and change.

Disenfranchised grief becomes even more confusing when the man is grieving not just the fallout from the infidelity, but also how he felt during the infidelity itself. Before discovery or disclosure, he may have experienced feelings of desire, power, or renewed energy, which temporarily alleviated the discontent or dissatisfaction he felt in his primary relationship. These positive emotions, however fleeting or based on unhealthy choices, can create a deep internal conflict after the affair is exposed. The man may feel ashamed for having enjoyed aspects of the affair and may struggle with reconciling these past feelings with the guilt and remorse he's expected to show in the aftermath.

This creates a layered and unspoken grief. On one hand, he may be mourning the excitement, validation, or sense of escape that the affair provided—experiences that might have felt like a lifeline in moments of personal or relational dissatisfaction. On the other hand, he is forced to confront the devastating consequences of those actions, leading to an internal battle between acknowledging the emotional relief he felt and recognizing the immense harm he caused. This complexity makes it even harder to fully process his grief, as it feels forbidden to express any sense of loss over something so destructive. Culturally, there is little room for men to openly discuss the positive emotions they experienced during the affair without being harshly judged, further deepening their disenfranchised grief.

Therapy often becomes the only space where these conflicting emotions can be explored, but even there, it can be difficult for men to admit that they are mourning how they felt during the infidelity. There is an expectation to focus on the hurt caused, which is essential for repair, but it often leaves little room for them to process the complexity of their own emotional experience. Without acknowledging this part of the grief, men can struggle with feelings of guilt, confusion, and shame that linger beneath the surface, preventing them from fully understanding the emotional drivers of their behavior. This makes authentic healing and growth more challenging, as they are not just grieving the loss of the relationship, but also the temporary emotional escape that the affair once provided.

DISENFRANCHISED GRIEF IN THERAPY

Therapists working with men who have committed infidelity need to carefully balance accountability with compassion. It's crucial to help these men acknowledge their grief, even when it's unrecognized or socially invalidated. When men are given space to process the complicated emotions that come with infidelity—beyond guilt and shame—they can begin to understand the deeper losses they're experiencing. By addressing their disenfranchised grief, they can move beyond self-punishment and work toward genuine change, repair, and emotional growth.

Working with men in individual therapy versus couples therapy requires distinct approaches to address disenfranchised grief. In individual therapy, the focus is often on creating a safe, non-judgmental space where the man can explore his own emotional complexities without the pressure of having to focus on demonstrating accountability or the emotions of his partner. This setting allows him to unpack his feelings of loss, shame, and even the conflicting emotions he experienced during the affair, including moments of empowerment, joy, excitement, or relief. The therapist can help him process these layers of grief more fully, working through how they connect to his sense of self, unmet needs, and the discontent that led to the infidelity. In individual sessions, men can also explore personal growth, learning healthier ways to cope with emotional challenges that don't involve betrayal or avoidance.

Working in Couples Therapy

In couples therapy, the dynamic shifts significantly, as the primary focus is on the relationship's recovery and rebuilding trust. The therapist must balance the needs of both partners, helping the man take responsibility for his actions while also validating the deep pain experienced by the betrayed partner. The space for the man's personal grief may be more limited at the beginning of couple's work, as the priority is often on repairing the emotional connection and addressing the hurt caused. Here, the therapist works to facilitate productive communication, ensuring the man expresses remorse in a way that fosters healing while guiding him through the process of empathizing with his partner's pain. His disenfranchised grief may be touched upon, but only insofar as it contributes to the couple's understanding of how the infidelity occurred, and this may make it harder for him to fully process his own emotional struggles. Couples therapy can, therefore, feel more constrained for the man, as it requires balancing individual healing with the collective goal of restoring the relationship.

As couples therapy progresses beyond the initial crisis stage, the focus naturally begins to shift. In the early stages, the primary goal is often to help the man fully acknowledge the pain he caused and take responsibility for his actions. This is crucial for rebuilding trust and validating his betrayed partner's emotions. However, once this foundation is established, therapy should gradually move toward a more collaborative phase, where the couple works together to understand the larger dynamics that contributed to the breakdown of their relationship. Rather than keeping the conflict centered between them—where blame and hurt dominate—therapy becomes about moving that conflict to a space where both partners can objectively explore it together.

At this point, the goal is to help the couple join forces in examining the deeper issues that have shaped their relationship. This might include looking at unmet emotional needs, communication patterns, past unresolved hurts, or even individual vulnerabilities that contributed to the distance between them. By shifting from a blame-focused dialogue to one that is more exploratory and curious, both partners can begin to see their relationship as something they can actively work on together. This collaborative approach fosters empathy, as each person gains a clearer understanding of how their personal dynamics influenced the relationship's trajectory. The shift from "me versus you" to "us versus the problem" is crucial for long-term healing, helping the couple grow together rather than remain stuck in cycles of conflict.

In couples therapy, I help move the conflict of infidelity from being something that sits between the partners to something they can explore together by using a physical object as a visual metaphor. I'll ask the couple to choose something in the room—like a plant or a clock— and then I'll point to it and say, "That thing.... Let's join together and talk about that." This simple shift helps them externalize the issue, so they're no longer facing off against each other but instead standing side by side, both looking at the dynamic of the infidelity as a shared challenge. By giving them a physical reminder of what it feels like to approach the problem as a team, they can begin to see the conflict not as something dividing them, but as something they can jointly understand and address. This method reinforces the idea of working together to explore the dynamics of their relationship, rather than being locked in opposition.

My philosophy challenges the common belief that love and sex are the glue that holds relationships together. While these are important components, the true glue in a relationship is intention and curiosity, as I talk about in greater detail in my first book, *Couples by Intention*. At this point in therapy, when a couple is trying to repair their bond after infidelity, these two qualities are deeply tested. Acting with intention means making deliberate, conscious choices that align with a desired outcome, rather than reacting impulsively or escaping discomfort, as often happens during infidelity. When someone cheats, their actions are typically made without full awareness or accountability, driven more by avoidance, immediate gratification, or emotional relief. The lack of intention leads to decisions that destabilize the relationship, leaving a trail of unprocessed emotions and unmet needs.

Being intentional in a relationship means showing up with full awareness, not only of one's own desires but also of how actions affect the partner and the relationship as a whole. It requires a conscious effort to reflect on what both partners want to create in their relationship, and to choose actions that foster connection, healing, and mutual respect. In contrast to the impulsivity and immediate gratification of infidelity, intention invites thoughtfulness and foresight. This shift is particularly difficult in the aftermath of betrayal, where emotional wounds are fresh, but it is essential for rebuilding trust and making active choices that support a healthier, more connected future.

Curiosity, too, is crucial because it involves challenging assumptions and being willing to sit with uncertainty. When couples operate on assumptions—about what the other person is thinking, feeling, or expecting or what they think about themselves and what may be available to them—they often close off opportunities for deeper understanding. Curiosity means embracing the possibility that we don't know everything about ourselves or our partner and being open to discovering new information. This openness allows for richer conversations, greater empathy, and more creative solutions to relational problems. In the context of infidelity recovery, curiosity lets the couple explore the deeper dynamics of their relationship, rather than jumping to conclusions or reverting to old patterns. It creates space for both partners to grow individually and together, which is essential for long-term healing and intimacy.

The work of couples therapy is to guide both partners in strategically using intention and curiosity to make healthy forward movement in their relationship. This involves helping each person become more mindful of their choices and actions, making sure they align with their shared goals for the relationship. By cultivating intention, partners can move away from reactive or impulsive behaviors and instead focus on actions that foster healing, trust, and connection. At the same time, therapy encourages curiosity—both about themselves and each other. This means challenging assumptions, asking deeper questions, and being open to discovering new dynamics or patterns that may have gone unnoticed. Together, intention and curiosity provide the framework for navigating conflict, understanding unmet needs, and creating a future where both partners feel seen, valued, and invested in the relationship's growth.

WORKING WITH MEN IN INDIVIDUAL THERAPY

Assessing disenfranchised grief in individual therapy with men who have committed infidelity requires a nuanced approach that explores both the overt and hidden emotional experiences they may be struggling with. The first step is creating a safe, non-judgmental space where the client feels comfortable discussing his emotions, especially those that might feel conflicting or socially unacceptable. Start by gently exploring the feelings of loss that may have arisen after the discovery or disclosure of the affair. This might include obvious losses, like the potential end of the relationship or trust, but also less acknowledged losses, such as the man's sense of self or the emotional relief he felt during the affair. Asking open-ended questions like, "What has changed for you since the affair was discovered?", "Who knows, and how are you responding to that?" or "What do you feel you've lost in this process?" can open the door to these deeper discussions.

It's also important to probe for feelings of shame, guilt, and regret, which are often closely tied to disenfranchised grief. These emotions may mask or complicate the grieving process, as men might feel that they don't have the right to mourn anything related to the affair. A key part of this assessment involves validating the client's experience, while helping him recognize that grief can coexist with accountability. For instance, you might ask, "Are there parts of your experience that feel difficult to grieve because of the hurt that's been caused?" or "How does the shame you feel affect your ability to reflect on what you've lost?" These kinds of inquiries help distinguish between guilt over the betrayal and the deeper, often unspoken, grief over the personal consequences of the infidelity.

Next, assess how much of the man's grief is related to the positive feelings he may have experienced during the affair. Many men feel desired, empowered, or reinvigorated during the infidelity, and these emotions can create a complicated sense of loss after the affair is exposed. In therapy, it's essential to ask about these experiences in a way that normalizes the conflicting emotions without condoning the behavior. Questions like, "What did the affair provide for you emotionally that you're now missing?" or "How do you feel about the emotional experiences you had during the affair?" can help uncover this aspect of disenfranchised grief. These emotions are often buried under guilt and many men struggle to honestly name them, but they need to be processed to prevent lingering confusion or emotional disconnection.

It's also helpful to explore how social expectations and cultural norms contribute to the disenfranchised grief. Men who commit infidelity may feel that they are undeserving of sympathy or support, and that their only role now is to repair the damage caused to their partner. Assessing the impact of these external pressures is crucial in understanding why their grief may be disenfranchised. Questions like, "Do you feel like you're able to talk about your own emotions outside of this space?" or "What kind of responses do you get when you try to express what you're going through?" can illuminate the lack of social support that often accompanies this form of grief.

Finally, assess how this disenfranchised grief is affecting the man's behavior and emotional processing. Is he shutting down emotionally, avoiding difficult conversations, or becoming overly defensive in his relationship? By identifying how his unprocessed grief is manifesting in his actions, you can begin to guide him toward healthier coping strategies. Explore whether he feels disconnected from his own emotional experience, or if he's struggling to reconcile his sense of self with the actions he's taken. Questions like, "How do you feel your emotions are influencing your decisions right now?" or "What do you notice about the way you handle conflict since the affair?" help link his grief to his current functioning, offering a path toward more intentional, mindful healing.

Even as a relationship heals from infidelity, disenfranchised grief can linger in the form of residual grief and anxiety, affecting the partner who committed the betrayal. For example, a man may still feel a sense of loss over the life he once had, not just in terms of the relationship, but also the emotional relief or validation he experienced during the affair. This grief can be hard to express because it feels inappropriate, given the hurt he caused, but it doesn't just disappear once the relationship starts to mend. He might feel a lingering sadness about how the affair ended abruptly, or even about losing a sense of personal freedom, even as he knows his relationship is moving forward. These unspoken feelings can show up in subtle ways, like moments of melancholy or detachment during what should be positive steps in the relationship's recovery.

Residual grief can also make the man hesitant to speak up for himself in the relationship, especially if he fears triggering his partner's anger or reopening emotional wounds. As the relationship heals, he may still carry a sense of guilt and responsibility for the pain he caused, which can lead to a reluctance to assert his own needs or feelings. He might worry that expressing frustration, dissatisfaction, or even a personal boundary could be interpreted as selfish or insensitive, especially given the emotional volatility that often follows infidelity. For instance, he may avoid bringing up a concern about the relationship or his emotional state because he fears it will reignite the pain or cause his partner to feel invalidated, which is too overwhelming for him to face.

This dynamic often leaves the man in a delicate emotional space, where he's caught between wanting to be fully present in the healing process and feeling like his own voice is no longer allowed to have weight. His residual grief may tell him that he doesn't have the right to ask for anything, given the hurt he's caused, so he stays quiet to avoid conflict. The fear of stepping on emotional triggers or making his partner angry can lead to a sense of disempowerment, where his role in the relationship becomes overly focused on damage control. This avoidance, though meant to prevent further harm, can stall genuine healing, as open communication and mutual expression are essential to rebuilding a healthy relationship. His inability or fear of coming forward with his emotional needs and experiences can leave the betrayed partner feeling that she is just being pacified and he can't or doesn't really want to recommit.

Residual anxiety is another form of disenfranchised grief that can persist as the relationship heals. The man may constantly fear that his past choices will resurface or worry that the trust he broke will never fully be restored. He might be anxious about making the wrong move, hyperaware of his actions, or overly cautious in his interactions, trying to avoid triggering any more hurt. For example, even after months of progress, he might feel a spike of anxiety when his partner checks his phone or brings up the past, fearing it could unravel everything. This anxiety, driven by unprocessed grief, can quietly undermine the relationship's growth if left unaddressed, making it harder for him to fully relax and trust in the healing process.

Residual anxiety can make the man fearful of discussing the infidelity, especially as time passes and his memory of events becomes less precise. He may worry that if he doesn't recount the experience in the exact same way every time, his partner will challenge him, suspecting that he's hiding something or being dishonest. This fear of being seen as deceptive can cause him to avoid conversations about the affair altogether, which can stall the healing process. There is a reality, however, that memory naturally shifts over time—nuances of events may become less clear, details may blur, and emotions may change in their intensity. Despite this normal process, the man may feel immense pressure to remember every aspect perfectly, as any variation could be interpreted as evidence of ongoing secrecy. This anxiety can keep him in a heightened state of defensiveness, afraid that one small inconsistency could unravel the fragile trust that's been rebuilt, leaving him trapped between his desire to heal and his fear of reigniting suspicion.

PUBLIC SHAMING

The public shaming of an affair can create profound disenfranchised grief, especially when the betrayal becomes known to children and family members. For the man who has committed the infidelity, the exposure of his actions to loved ones can leave him feeling as though his status with those closest to him is irreparably damaged. He may experience a deep sense of loss, not only in terms of the trust within his marriage but also in his relationships with his children, parents, or extended family. The affair, once known, can lead these loved ones to view him through the lens of betrayal, making it difficult for him to rebuild his identity within these circles. The grief he feels in losing his role as a respected father, son, or family member often goes unacknowledged, as the focus tends to remain on the pain of the betrayed partner. This disenfranchised grief is compounded by the challenge of regaining the respect and trust of those who may see him as permanently tainted.

Bringing the affair recovery back to the intimacy of the marriage becomes particularly difficult when family members are involved. Once the affair is known, loved ones may feel that they have a right to insert themselves into the couple's healing process, offering opinions or advice—whether welcomed or not. While this may be done out of concern, it can also add another layer of pressure on the man, who is already grappling with his own guilt and the emotional labor of repairing the relationship. Holding boundaries with family and close friends becomes essential but challenging, as they may struggle to step back once they're aware of the infidelity. The couple, especially the man, may feel caught between managing the fallout within their marriage and managing the expectations or judgments of others. This intrusion makes it harder to keep the focus on their intimate healing process and can intensify the man's sense of isolation in his grief. It is important to be able to thank loved ones for their concern and support while reminding them that "We are working through this together and are keeping the work within the marriage."

In friend groups, public knowledge of the affair can lead to social distancing, as friends may start to withdraw from the man or the couple altogether. Some friends might feel uncomfortable being caught in the middle, while others may pass judgment and side with the betrayed partner. The man may find himself losing not only his marital relationship but also his broader social circle, which can exacerbate his sense of grief and isolation. Friends who once provided support may no longer feel comfortable maintaining closeness, further disenfranchising the man's experience of loss. This social fallout can create a secondary grief—one of lost friendships and community—which may be difficult for him to process, especially if he feels undeserving of sympathy.

When the affair becomes known in the workplace or broadcast on social media, the public shaming can reach a devastating level. At work, the man might face challenges to his respectability, promotions, or even his ability to maintain employment. Colleagues and supervisors may view him through the lens of his personal life, questioning his judgment or trustworthiness. In more severe cases, workplace gossip or a tarnished reputation can have lasting career impacts, adding financial stress to the emotional turmoil he's already experiencing. When a betrayed partner broadcasts the infidelity on social media, it empowers others to openly demean, shame, and belittle the man in a very public way. This amplification of the shaming makes it nearly impossible for him to process his grief privately. The more public the affair becomes, the more complicated it is for him to address his own pain, as the social narrative often leaves little room for his feelings, forcing him to retreat further into isolation while his grief remains unacknowledged and unresolved.

PART

II

▼

RESEARCH

∽

Happiness is found in healing, not in seeking revenge for infidelity.

—Author Unknown

5

▼

THE ARC
OF INFIDELITY
RECOVERY

The journey of infidelity recovery is long but can have a predictable arc to it. When people start working with me, especially if they start close to discovery or disclosure, they want someone who will tell them everything will be okay. If they don't start therapy until a while after discovery or disclosure, they are looking for someone to break the painful dynamic that seems unbreakable and unchangeable. Either way, there can be a path forward.

In order to explore the true fracture of infidelity, we have to take a high-level look at the journey before we move into the details. When the reality of infidelity begins to be known, both partners can have extreme reactions. It is a time of extreme emotions, lack of hope, and erratic confusion. Believing there is a path forward seems almost impossible. They want to feel secure again, but security is a long journey.

Security is a long journey because there are three distinct relationship dynamics that must be reconciled after an infidelity: forgiveness, trust, and security. They are distinct but interconnected phenomena that require time, patience, and effort to develop and sustain in the aftermath of infidelity. Each dynamic must be understood uniquely and understood by how it connects to the others. Without forgiveness and trust, therefore, there is no security.

Forgiveness requires awareness, the awareness of what is and what has happened. It is the reason why disclosure is important. Disclosure is knowing what *is* important—the whys, whens, with whom, frequency, and more—while not getting drowned in what is not important—the specifics of a particular act or communication. Focusing on what is important allows each partner to get a grasp on the reality they are facing. Forgiveness is for yourself, not the other person. It is a kind of awareness that allows you to make clear choices so you can start to break down the walls that keep you locked in. When you accept fully what has happened and stop living in the hope that it will or can be different, you can accept the work in front of you which allows you to make the forward movement you want.

Trust is a decision. Even though core trust has been broken there will be many areas in your relationship where trust still exists. In other words, the decision to trust is not binary. It's not all or nothing. Trust is placed in many areas, but not in others. For example, if your partner has cheated on you, do you have trust that he can still be a good father? That he will go to work and be a good provider? Finding the places where trust has not been broken is key for trust in the broken areas to be repaired. Being able to identify the areas where trust is not broken helps to modulate the pain and create a space where some consistency can be found. What will support this rebuilding of trust is your own and your partner's consistency in recovery work over time. When consistent effort over time is made in the areas of broken trust, you and your partner can make more decisions to trust again.

Whereas forgiveness begins with awareness and knowledge, and trust is a decision, security is a feeling. You and your partner can reestablish a sense of security but it requires a significant amount of time and work by both parties. Security means you will have a sense of feeling safe and confident in your relationship. Often the feeling of security begins to emerge without clear awareness that it is happening because both partners are focused on the problems and the emotional challenges of the moment. Often people will say that when they feel secure, they will make the decision to trust, and then they will forgive. However, it actually works in the opposite direction: when you become aware and begin to accept the realities you have been confronted with, you can make decisions to trust in more areas (after periods of consistent recovery work). Then, after you make those decisions to trust, you begin to feel secure. You cannot feel secure if you have not made the decision to trust.

THE PHASES OF INFIDELITY RECOVERY

It is important to know what the journey you are embarking on will look like. Although no one can predict the specifics, there is a general process that partners can expect if both are doing the work to rebuild the relationship. Here are the phases I have identified through my decades of working with couples on infidelity recovery, and the national study I described in Chapters 3 and 6.

- ▼ Crisis
- ▼ Keeping Vigil and Regrounding
- ▼ Reconnecting
- ▼ Retrusting
- ▼ Forward Planning

CRISIS

The Crisis phase of infidelity recovery is an incredibly intense and emotionally charged period during which both partners can feel overwhelmed by a whirlwind of conflicting emotions.

During this time, it's common for clear thinking to be clouded by shock, anger, sadness, and confusion, making it difficult to know how to proceed. Black-and-white thinking begins to take over. This is usually the time individuals and couples turn to therapy, desperately seeking guidance and answers on how to move forward. They may come to the therapist with the hope that someone can save their relationship—or at least navigate them through the chaos they're experiencing. Sometimes one partner is looking for a therapist to validate them against the other so their feelings seem more justified. Their need for clarity is immense as they struggle to understand what has happened, how to deal with the pain, and whether their relationship can survive. A therapist in this phase often becomes a critical resource, helping them to process their emotions, manage the intense challenges, and start to piece together a path toward healing. This phase of the work is centered on grounding both partners and getting an honest and realistic understanding of what happened before and during the discovery or disclosure process.

What makes Crisis more difficult is disclosure by a thousand cuts. The betrayed partner often wants all the information up front, honestly, and without hesitation. Full disclosure without editing—no matter how lascivious the details. The desire for full disclosure often stems from a need to regain a sense of control and clarity. The betrayal has shattered trust and left the betrayed partner with countless unanswered questions. Full disclosure, no matter how painful, provides a way for the betrayed partner to understand the full extent of what happened, which can help in piecing together a shattered reality. Without complete honesty, the betrayed partner may fear there is more to the story than they've been told and be left feeling they are waiting for the other shoe to drop, which can prolong the healing process.

The betrayed partner, after discovering the infidelity, often turns to intense surveillance of their partner, tracking location, checking phones, emails, and social media in an effort to regain a sense of safety and control. This behavior is driven by a combination of hurt and anxiety, as they desperately seek reassurance that the betrayal won't happen again. However, instead of fostering security, this constant monitoring can deepen feelings of mistrust and create a tense, hostile environment. Both partners may feel trapped—one in guilt and loss of privacy, the other in a cycle of fear and uncertainty—making true healing even more difficult to achieve.

Thus, full disclosure is often seen by the betrayed partner as a crucial step toward rebuilding trust. The act of the betraying partner coming clean about everything, no matter how difficult it is to share, can demonstrate their willingness to be transparent and committed to repairing the relationship. It also allows the betrayed partner to assess the situation fully, helping them make informed decisions about whether they can move forward together. While hearing the details can be incredibly painful, many betrayed partners find that knowing the truth, even in its most uncomfortable forms, is a necessary part of the healing process.

It is important to note that full disclosure does not mean the betrayed partner learning the specifics of sexual acts, or even the exact words used in communications with the affair partner. In my experience counseling countless couples recovering from infidelity, learning the intimate details of the infidelity, particularly details of the sexual acts or language, can often do more harm than good for the betrayed partner. These vivid and explicit details can create distorted mental images that are hard to recover from, leading to intrusive thoughts and a heightened sense of emotional distress. Rather than aiding in the healing process, this deep dive into the sexual specifics of the affair can amplify the pain. Instead, focusing on the critical factors of places, times, and frequency of the infidelity, as well as the why, how it made the betrayer feel, and what he was thinking about before, during, and after, can provide the necessary context without delving into details that magnify the trauma. Understanding the broader patterns of the affair helps the betrayed partner grasp the extent of implications of the betrayal without getting lost in specifics that can lead to obsessive thoughts or comparisons, ultimately allowing for a more manageable and constructive path toward healing.

The betrayer often wants to mitigate the truth, reduce the damage, looking for a place to find security in the midst of extreme vulnerability. A betraying partner often struggles to give full disclosure because of deep feelings of guilt and shame. Admitting the details of an affair forces them to confront their actions head-on, which can be excruciating. They may feel horrified by their own behavior, and by revealing the full truth, they risk damaging the image their partner has of them even further. This sense of guilt can make it difficult to be completely honest, as they fear that sharing everything will cause irreparable harm. Trying to minimize the story often has a feeling of keeping it containable. There's often a fear of losing their partner, their family, and the life they have built. By keeping certain details hidden, they may believe they're sparing their partner unnecessary pain, hoping to protect what's left of the relationship or reduce the fallout from their actions.

What I have found, however, is that withholding the full necessary truth (places, times, frequency of the infidelity, as well as the why, how it made the betrayer feel, and what he was thinking before, during, and after) keeps the betraying partner trapped in secrecy, creating additional internal conflict. While they may fear the consequences of full disclosure, holding onto the hidden details weighs heavily on them. The burden of constantly lying, covering up, or worrying about the truth coming out can take an emotional toll, leaving them feeling isolated and anxious. Paradoxically, once the secret is out, they may experience great relief. The betraying partner no longer has to live in fear of being found out. While the fallout is painful, they can finally start to deal with the consequences openly. This ambivalence—the desire to hide the truth to preserve their relationship contrasted with the relief that comes from being honest—is a difficult emotional tug-of-war, leaving the man torn between protecting himself, and facing the truth head-on.

KEEPING VIGIL AND REGROUNDING

In this phase of recovery, the betrayed partner is starting to breathe again and re-engage in basic life activities. However, intrusive thoughts and feelings remain constant in every situation. Triggers are every-where. Reactivity remains high. The keeping vigil and regrounding phase shifts the partners' focus to opening communication, trust, and creating a new sense of stability in the relationship. The goal in this phase is for the man to establish consistency. He must demonstrate reliability and transparency to begin mending the betrayed partner's broken trust. Open lines of communication are essential, allowing both partners to express their feelings, needs, and fears honestly. This phase is about finding a balance between addressing the pain of the past and creating a sense of security for the future. It is a delicate process that requires patience, commitment, and a shared willingness to explore whether the relationship can be rebuilt on a new foundation of honesty and accountability.

This phase can be particularly challenging for men because they often fear that anything they say or do might cause further damage. Their need to fix and stabilize becomes deeply confused. There is a tendency to walk on eggshells, afraid that any misstep could reignite their partner's pain and anger. Thus, they can no longer stabilize in the ways they are accustomed to doing. Their fear can make it difficult to engage fully in the necessary conversations, leading to avoidance or defensiveness instead of the open communication that is needed for healing. What may be constant emotional assault from their partner—expressions of hurt, anger, and mistrust—can feel overwhelming. Men may struggle with the intensity of these emotions, wanting relief from the situation yet unsure how to achieve it without making things worse.

On top of this, being in a one-down position, where they are no longer seen as the equal partner but rather as the one who caused the pain, can be deeply unsettling. This role reversal can challenge their sense of identity and self-worth, as they grapple with shame, guilt, and powerlessness. For men who are used to being seen as strong or in control, this shift can be particularly difficult to navigate. They may struggle with how to effectively support their partner while also dealing with their own emotional turmoil.

Men must maintain a particular focus for this complex and painful phase of their recovery. They must focus on what I call "keeping vigil," which means taking a lead role in acknowledging the infidelity and its impact daily. This means not just waiting for the betrayed partner to bring it up; instead, it's about the man taking the initiative to address the pain and reality of the situation from the woman's perspective. By doing this, the man shows that he is fully engaged in the healing process and that he understands the gravity of what has happened. When men don't bring up the infidelity on their own, the woman often feels like she is carrying the emotional burden alone. This can lead to her feeling frustrated, isolated, resentful, and that her pain is not understood or taken seriously.

The reality is the betrayed partner is likely to bring up the infidelity frequently, especially in the early stages of recovery. If the man avoids these conversations or waits for his partner to initiate them, it can come across as though he is trying to sweep the issue under the rug or is not fully committed to the healing process. This can deepen the mistrust and make it harder for the relationship to recover. On the other hand, when the man consistently and mindfully brings up the topic himself, it reassures his partner that he is aware of the pain and is not shying away from the hard work of rebuilding trust. It shows that he is not just trying to move past the infidelity but is actively engaging with the reality of the situation and taking responsibility for the ongoing emotional process.

By showing this daily mindfulness, the man can help create a safer emotional space for his partner where she feels heard, understood, and supported. This consistent effort is a way of demonstrating that he is fully present in the relationship and is committed to making amends, no matter how uncomfortable or difficult they may be. Keeping vigil in this way is not mostly about addressing the past, although it may feel that way. It is about building a foundation for a future where both partners can eventually feel secure and connected again.

This process of keeping vigil is particularly difficult for many men because it requires a level of vulnerability that goes against the norms of hegemonic masculinity, which often dictate that men should be stoic, strong, and emotionally reserved. Society has long taught men to suppress their emotions, especially those that involve pain, guilt, or fear, as these are often seen as signs of weakness. However, in the context of infidelity recovery, truly engaging with their partner's pain requires men to confront these emotions head-on and openly discuss them—a practice that many are not well-versed in. This act of being emotionally present and showing vulnerability can feel uncomfortable and even foreign, as it challenges the deeply ingrained belief that men must always be in control. Yet this vulnerability is essential for rebuilding trust and connection, making it a crucial, though challenging, step in the healing process.

It is essential for the man to approach the vigil primarily from his partner's point of view, focusing on her pain, her needs, and her perspective. This demonstrates that he truly understands the impact of his actions and is committed to addressing the harm he has caused. If he shifts the conversation to his own guilt, loss, or perspective, he risks placing an additional burden on his partner, essentially asking her to help solve his emotional struggles at a time when she is already overwhelmed by her own. It is important for the man to remember that there will be a time soon when he can bring his struggles to the conversation and ask her to be aware and support him, but that can only come after she has felt his awareness of what he has done. By centering his actions and conversations at this time on her experience, he shows that he is prioritizing her well-being and is dedicated to making amends, which is crucial to rebuilding trust and moving forward. At the same time, he must do his own individual work to unpack his experience. This is why for the man, being in individual therapy in this phase can provide him crucial support and space to unpack his feelings and experience.

It is my experience that when working with men during infidelity recovery, they struggle with the concept of keeping vigil. I spend an extraordinary amount of time helping men learn how to use curiosity as a strategic tool in their work. I talk to them about how to do something every day that shows their partner that they are aware of the pain she is holding. Perhaps it is a note or a card every day expressing his awareness. It is his ability to bring up the infidelity so she does not have to bring it up to him. Instead of asking questions such as "How are you doing today?", learning to ask questions such as "How has your pain shifted since you learned about my infidelity?" "Where are your triggers coming from now?" "Have you seen the efforts from me that you need to see?" Keeping vigil also includes the moments when you might be watching television and the storyline includes infidelity. This moment can be deeply triggering. Knowing that pausing the remote and addressing the moment in real-time, as well as acknowledging awareness of the discomfort, is an important step in keeping vigil. The key to keeping a successful vigil is for the man to bring the infidelity conversation and awareness to the table, not avoid it, and not make his partner responsible for driving the recovery conversations.

Regrounding is the delicate process of beginning to find a new way to coexist as a couple and rebuild a relationship that has been deeply shaken. This phase often begins when the couple decides to start working together again after the initial shock and separation, which might include the man moving out of the house or sleeping on the couch. These physical separations can appropriately symbolize the emotional distance created by the betrayal. Regrounding is about beginning to bridge that emotional distance. It's creating a space where both partners can begin to feel safe and connected again, even if the dynamics of the relationship have fundamentally changed. This process requires patience, understanding, and a commitment to redefining how they interact with, communicate, and support one another moving forward.

A crucial part of regrounding is agreeing on new rules and boundaries that will guide the relationship in this new phase. This might include establishing clear expectations around communication, transparency, and behaviors that support trust-building. Both partners need to actively participate in this process, ensuring that the boundaries reflect the needs of the betrayed partner while also being fair and manageable for both. The goal is to create a shared understanding of what is required to heal and move forward, and to lay the groundwork for a relationship that, while different than before, can still be meaningful and fulfilling. Regrounding is not just about restoring what was lost; it's about constructing a new foundation based on honesty, respect, and mutual effort.

A confusing aspect for many couples after the discovery or disclosure of infidelity is the shifting dynamic of sexual intimacy. If sex was distant or nonexistent prior, the fear that it can never come back can be a daunting thought. If sex was good and consistent prior, both partners may have conflicting feelings about reengaging in physical, sexual, or emotional intimacy as they grapple with the pain of betrayal. There may be a deep uncertainty about how to approach these moments, fearing that any attempt to reconnect could be misconstrued or rejected, resulting in emotional and relational disorientation. Both partners can lose their footing here.

In some couples, there is a noticeable uptick in sexual activity after the infidelity is out, even if sexual activity had been lacking for some time. This increase can be driven by the betrayed partner's attempt to demonstrate what was at stake and what the relationship could have been as they attempt to reassert their value and connection in a way that feels tangible. This phenomenon, which some of my clients have referred to as "fucking my man faithful," can create a complex emotional landscape. The betrayed partner might be using sex as a means of reaffirming their bond and proving their commitment, while the man may experience guilt and confusion about the sudden shift in the dynamics in the face of the emotional turmoil that continues.

This sexual intensity is often time-limited, as each partner begins to feel reconnected. While one partner may feel the increase in activity feels confirming and a sign of security, the other might find it a confusing responsibility to avoid more conflict. As the reality of day-to-day responsibility sets in, and as more time passes from the moment of discovery or disclosure, sexual activity will often revert to what was experienced previously. The return of a more normal sexual frequency can often be confusing, with partners feeling torn between a desire to maintain the heightened sexual activity and a return to something more sustainable. Being able to talk about what sex looks like post-discovery is an important exploration that can help ground both partners in how to connect in this phase.

RECONNECTING

The reconnecting phase marks a period of relative stability in the aftermath of infidelity, where the daily eruptions and triggers that once seemed relentless begin to settle. While both partners remain acutely aware of the fracture in their relationship and the ongoing emotional pain, they have managed to establish a functional stasis that allows them to move forward. This phase represents a shift from the intense, immediate crisis to a more manageable routine where the immediate turmoil has lessened, though the underlying issues of trust and hurt are still very much present. As they transition into this phase, the process of keeping vigil evolves; it becomes less about daily confrontation and more about maintaining ongoing efforts to rebuild and sustain trust. Despite the relative calm, the emotional scars and lack of trust continue to influence their interactions, requiring continued vigilance and commitment from both partners.

During the reconnecting phase, the focus shifts to intense, purposeful work on the relationship. The objective is not simply to return to how things were before the infidelity but to forge a completely new relationship built on a foundation of new skills, agreements, boundaries, and structures. This period involves actively learning and implementing healthier communication strategies, setting clear boundaries, and developing a deeper understanding of each other's needs and vulnerabilities. There is a rediscovery of who each partner is and where they are in the recovery process. This requires that each partner does their own deep work to better understand themselves, their needs, and their triggers. Both partners must engage in honest dialogue and work collaboratively to create a framework that supports mutual respect and trust. By establishing these new patterns and agreements, they can transform the relationship into one that acknowledges the past while moving forward with greater awareness and commitment. This process is crucial for developing a partnership that is resilient and fulfilling, distinct from the relationship that existed before the betrayal.

This phase can be particularly challenging because the man is likely still feeling stuck in a one-down position, hesitant to be fully vulnerable now that the initial "heat" of the crisis has subsided. The emotional intensity of the earlier stages, which kept him on high alert and actively engaged, has decreased, leaving him grappling with lingering feelings of shame and inadequacy. At the same time, the betrayed partner may have concerns that the reduced intensity could lead the man to become complacent or less focused on the ongoing work of recovery. There's a fear that without the constant pressure of immediate emotional upheaval, he might slack off in his efforts to rebuild trust and address the issues at hand. This dynamic creates a complex environment where both partners must navigate the balance between maintaining necessary vigilance and adapting to a more stable, yet still fragile, relationship.

This is the phase when I like to introduce the concept of being a good manipulator. When I first introduce the concept, there is an expected scowl of disdain. It is important to break down what a manipulator actually means. The root of the word comes from the Latin *manipulus* which means *handful*. So, the actual definition of the word *manipulate* means "having a handful" or "using your hands," thus controlling in a skillful manner. Let's correlate this to throwing clay on a potter's wheel. You must use your hands to work the clay. At first the clay is hard and needs water and kneading in your hands to soften. Then, you can throw it on the wheel and start to form the ball into the object of your choice.

Our relationship at this phase is like the clay. We must work it and get it into the right consistency and then start to form it into our finished product. We don't want to manipulate our relationships in an evil or hurtful manner, but to shape it *together*. If we both have our hands on the clay, we can start to form it into what we want as an end result. For this to be successful, we have to have an agreement on what we are making: a bowl? A vase? A plate? As long as we are in agreement, the emerging object will be successful. We must be communicating about the ongoing texture of the clay and the end product we agree to build.

It is not surprising that both partners would be hesitant to think of themselves as manipulators—especially in light of the pain and broken trust they are experiencing. However, it is this shift to engaging *together* in shaping the new relationship and not avoiding, even though broken trust remains, that becomes critical. Engaging together without trust can seem like a big ask, but it is the first step to rebuilding, which is what the couple wants if they have come this far and put in this much effort. When this is done with some consistency from both partners, it opens them up to stepping into the next phase: retrusting.

RETRUSTING

Rebuilding trust after infidelity is a painfully slow process, and one that both partners may struggle to fully comprehend. When trust is first broken, it can feel irreparable, leaving both partners wondering if it's even possible to regain what is lost. The partner who was betrayed may wrestle with doubt, anger, resentment, and strong skepticism, while the one who was unfaithful often struggles with guilt, remorse, and a confusion coming from the reality that efforts to repair and comfort are often met with harshness. What makes this process so difficult is the understanding that trust won't be restored overnight. It requires consistent effort and patience with neither partner being at their best.

As a reminder, trust at its core is a decision. It's not just about whether one partner is worthy of trust but also about whether the other is willing to re-open their heart to the possibility of trusting again. The decision to trust by the betrayed partner demands consistency from the betraying partner—small, intentional actions repeated over time that show the commitment to change. It's not enough for the unfaithful partner to simply "do everything" to fix things; he must be curious and intentional about what their betrayed partner truly needs. Without that understanding, even the most well-intentioned actions can miss the mark, leaving the betrayed partner feeling uncared for, reinjured, and growing in resentment.

This is where the work deepens. Instead of guessing or overcompensating, the unfaithful partner must take the time to ask tough questions and really listen. What does their partner need in this moment? What does healing look like for them? How has the pain changed over time? What, where, and why are triggers showing up? These conversations are difficult and often uncomfortable, but they are essential. The betrayed partner may need emotional safety, reassurance, clarity, or specific boundaries that were never part of the relationship before. Understanding these needs requires vulnerability and the willingness to face uncomfortable truths together.

In many ways, this new chapter of the relationship becomes about continuing to keep vigil in new ways, showing up with consistency, honesty, and openness to the hard conversations, day after day. It's not about grand gestures or fixing things overnight; it's about making space for ongoing discussions to evolve. This can feel exhausting, especially for the unfaithful man, who might feel that he's already giving everything he knows how to give. And the reality is that, for many men, what they know to give is limited, as we learned from the theories discussed in Chapter 2. Many men were not raised and are not experienced in how to be emotionally vulnerable, communicate their feelings with words, and show curiosity when they feel a lack of safety. Hegemonic masculinity, social exchange, and feminist theories remind us that when men are taken out of their known patterns of behavior and response, they can lock up. The path to success is to help the man realize that he can find success when he can move through this challenging period. This is why this period is as much about understanding (for both the man and the woman) as it is about the man's effort. Without that deeper curiosity and intention, his actions may never fully resonate with her needs for healing and rebuilding trust.

The challenge of rebuilding trust becomes even more complicated when the betrayed partner struggles to acknowledge the efforts of the unfaithful man. This can be for many reasons, and it's not simply about a refusal to forgive. Past emotional injuries, unresolved childhood traumas, or even long-standing patterns in the relationship can create barriers to her seeing or accepting the change. For example, if the betrayed partner has been hurt before, has deep-rooted trust issues, high anxiety, or has been through a pattern of previous lies with this man, she may find it nearly impossible to accept the man's efforts at face value. The wounds from infidelity may tap into those older, unresolved pains, making the current betrayal feel even more overwhelming.

Additionally, there can be a sense of frustration and resentment if the betrayed partner feels they had repeatedly asked for change or therapy before the affair was known, only to be ignored or dismissed. When someone feels like they've been calling out for help in the relationship for a long time, and only after a betrayal does the partner seem to act, his efforts can feel too little, too late, or disingenuous. That history—of trying to push for repair before the crisis—can add layers of hurt and make it harder to accept that the man is now truly ready to do the work. The betrayed partner might think, "If only you had done this when I asked, we wouldn't be here," which adds to the complexity of the healing process.

Moreover, moral and ethical concerns can cloud the path to reconciliation. Infidelity can challenge deeply held values around commitment, honesty, respect, and how women should be valued and treated by men. The betrayed partner may question whether they can ever feel aligned with someone who has broken those values, making it difficult to see the man as changing. Even if the man is putting in significant work, these moral conflicts can keep the betrayed partner from fully embracing the possibility of trust again. In these cases, both individuals need to navigate not just the affair but these deeper, often unspoken issues that have been a part of their dynamic for a long time.

With the pain both partners are facing, moments of intimacy may be easily experienced, but then there is often a ricocheting experience back to the pain of infidelity. Intimacy thrives when there is a balance between safety and vulnerability. It's the delicate interplay between feeling secure enough to open up and being brave enough to share deep parts of ourselves. However, when trust has been broken, this balance is interrupted. If the need for safety begins to overpower vulnerability, the person closes themselves off, seeking protection and further pain. They might guard their emotions and distance themselves. On the other hand, if vulnerability outweighs safety, the person may feel exposed and triggered, unable to handle the emotional intensity of the situation. This imbalance can make intimacy feel either inaccessible or overwhelming. This dance of balance is experienced by both partners, but often hard to identify in the other because it can be expressed in different ways.

To rebuild trust during this fragile period, the man must go beyond surface-level efforts and learn new skills that allow him to better understand his own identity, communication style, and capacity for vulnerability. He must challenge beliefs he held about what it means to be a great partner. This requires deep introspection—realizing where he hasn't shown up in the relationship in ways that matter, the scripts that he has lived with, and the messages he has held about himself and the world. It's not just about grand gestures of apology or trying to "fix" things, which often comes across as him trying to fix his partner rather than addressing her pain. It's about learning to show up with emotional presence, empathy, and vulnerability in ways he may never have practiced before. He needs to understand what true connection looks like and how his actions, even before the infidelity, impacted the balance of safety and vulnerability between them. This is a huge ask because for many men, it counters every message they have lived since boyhood. When this form of masculinity and partnership is not taught and modeled, asking a man to make this change in the face of a fragile relationship can feel foreign and unreachable.

For this healing process to work, both partners must relearn that fragile balance between safety and vulnerability so decisions to trust again can be made. Consistency in words and actions is required. He needs to create an environment of emotional safety for his partner, so she can feel secure enough to express her needs, fears, and hopes without fear of being hurt again. At the same time, he must practice being open and vulnerable sharing his own emotional journey and how he is working to become a more present and committed partner.

He needs her to create a space where he can show up as a full human, with feelings, thoughts, and needs with trust that she will be open to them. Together, they will need to establish this new equilibrium, where both begin to feel safe enough to be vulnerable, but also brave enough to trust this safety will not be taken for granted. Only through this consistent rebalancing can intimacy, trust, and connection begin to be rebuilt.

As these shifts in the relationship begin to take place, they are often subtle and gradual. The constant intensity of triggers and fears starts to soften. While the pain of infidelity remains present, it no longer dominates every hour or interaction. There are moments where both partners begin to feel like they're functioning better together, as a team. They may start to have conversations or share experiences where the betrayal is not the central theme. These small wins—where the relationship feels less burdened by the affair and more focused on present life and future opportunities—are critical in rebuilding trust. It's not that the infidelity is forgotten, but it's no longer the most pressing or overwhelming part of their daily lives.

At this stage, the couple's focus shifts toward recalibrating their relationship, moving beyond just survival into a deeper partnership. For the man, this means learning to rise from the one-down position he may have been stuck in during the initial repair process. When the affair was first discovered, he likely found himself in a place where most of his actions, outside of his own individual therapy, were focused on what he could do to make things right and what would allow his partner to let him back in again. Staying stuck in that dynamic can create a challenging imbalance, where the man feels perpetually indebted or disempowered in the relationship.

Now, as both partners begin to recalibrate, it's about discovering what a true, equal partnership looks like. This requires the man to reclaim his own sense of self-worth and agency while maintaining the humility and vulnerability needed for continued growth. He has to learn how to contribute to the relationship in a way that isn't just about making amends but about being an active, emotional, whole-person partner. This shift is delicate; it's about moving from being reactive to proactive, from seeking forgiveness to co-creating a shared vision for the future. His partner has to decide to trust that when he advocates for himself, it is not the same self-serving partner she may have experienced in the past. Both partners have to negotiate what equality means—how they share emotional "jobs" in the relationship, make decisions, and support each other's growth. The true sign of growth in the relationship is when both partners are able to voice their needs, wants, and hopes in an equal fashion without fear of creating new injury or opening an old wound. Through this recalibration, the relationship transforms, becoming not just repaired but fundamentally redefined on a foundation of trust, openness, and mutual respect.

Even as the relationship begins to feel more secure and both partners grow more grounded in their connection, there remains a risk that life experiences can trigger old feelings reminiscent of the early stages of recovery. These moments may arise unexpectedly—a reminder of the affair, a stressful event, or even a misunderstanding that mirrors past wounds. In these instances, both partners might feel as if they are regressing, with old fears, insecurities, and doubts resurfacing. The betrayed partner may once again feel a sense of distrust or vulnerability, while the unfaithful partner might feel the weight of guilt or frustration, as if they're back at square one. This can be disheartening, especially when both have worked so hard to move forward.

However, the key difference at this stage is that, with time, both partners have developed new skills, communication tools, and emotional resilience. The trust they've painstakingly rebuilt and the emotional insight they've gained provide a foundation strong enough to withstand these setbacks. While the initial emotional response may feel overwhelming, it no longer defines the relationship. They've learned how to handle these triggers—how to talk through them, hold space for each other, and reassure one another that they're committed to continuing the journey of healing together.

Because of this, any temporary regression is not likely to stick as long as both partners are using their new skills. These difficult moments, though painful, become opportunities to practice the trust and vulnerability they've cultivated. Instead of falling back into old patterns of fear, blame, or avoidance, they can lean into the healthier dynamics they've established. They now have the confidence and understanding to rebound more quickly, moving through the emotional turbulence with a sense of shared purpose. Over time, these moments of challenge become less about re-living the past and more about reaffirming their growth. Each time they successfully navigate a setback, they reinforce their bond and continue building a partnership that's not just repaired but more resilient than before.

FORWARD PLANNING

When couples first confront infidelity, the shock and emotional pain for both partners can make it almost impossible to imagine any kind of future together. In that moment of discovery or disclosure, their world feels shattered, and the idea of planning ahead or rebuilding trust seems far out of reach. Hope can feel like a fragile, distant concept—something they want to believe in but can't. The uncertainty about whether they can move past the betrayal, combined with each partner's overwhelming emotions, makes it incredibly difficult to see beyond the immediate hurt. It's a slow, challenging process to hold onto the idea that healing is possible, especially when the future seems so uncertain.

After infidelity, when couples start realizing the stability that comes from growth and recovery, they often find themselves in the territory of creating what feels like a "new relationship" or "new marriage." This doesn't erase the past or mean that the hurt is gone, but it does signify a shift—a chance to redefine what they want this relationship to be moving forward. Part of this process is uncovering the *purpose* of this renewed commitment, which can look different for each partner. For one, it might be about feeling secure and appreciated emotionally, financially, or in other ways they haven't felt before. For the other, it may be about learning to feel genuinely connected and accountable to someone for the first time and finding new value in "family." These purposes don't need to align perfectly; rather, they offer a new foundation built on a deeper awareness of each partner's individual needs and boundaries.

Exploring these individual purposes opens up meaningful conversations about their future together, one in which each partner can articulate what this new relationship means to them. While they may have some overlapping goals, such as parenting, financial security, fostering trust, or emotional safety, the unique purposes each one brings create a sense of individual autonomy within their union. It can be a balancing act, recognizing and respecting their different intentions while finding areas where they're willing to grow together. This step is critical, as it not only shapes the shared vision of their future but also strengthens their ability to communicate openly. In honoring each other's separate yet complementary purposes, they forge a new relational dynamic that acknowledges both their individual growth and their commitment to building a more resilient partnership.

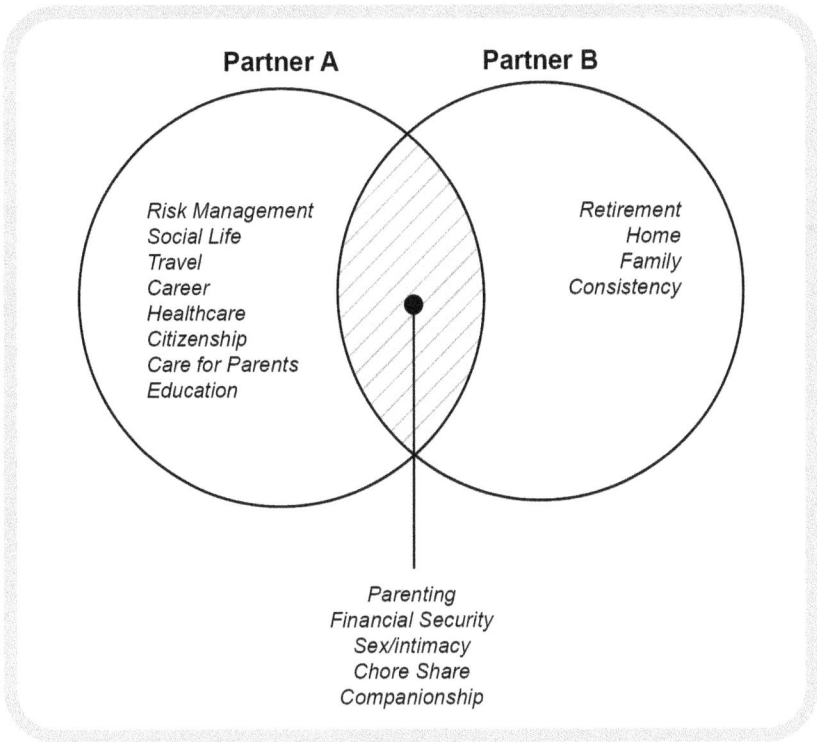

Figure 3: **Identifying Each Partner's Purpose of Relationship**

When couples approach each other with genuine curiosity in this new relationship phase, they open fresh avenues for communication, boundaries, and support structures that can make each partner feel truly seen and understood. Curiosity allows them to ask questions about each other's needs and desires without assuming they already know the answers. This can lead to surprising revelations—both about their partner and about their own previously unspoken needs. This type of exploration often brings a sense of closeness because each person learns that their partner is willing to meet them where they are, even if the path forward looks different than expected. As they communicate more openly, boundaries are redefined, and supportive structures begin to take shape that honor each partner's individuality within the relationship.

However, this level of curiosity and openness can also bring anxiety, especially when one partner realizes that the other's purposes or desires diverge from what they once believed or hoped. It can be unsettling to discover that each person's vision of the relationship has evolved in ways that don't perfectly align. But navigating this discomfort together can become a powerful growth experience, cultivating new skills, strength, and resiliency in the relationship. By leaning into these differences with respect and patience, couples not only develop the capacity to weather difficult emotions but also learn to embrace a more complex, authentic partnership. This growth lays the groundwork for a bond that's more adaptable and fulfilling, as each partner comes to recognize that it's their continued willingness to understand and support each other that sustains the relationship—not a rigid adherence to past expectations.

6

▼

INFIDELITY AND THE THERAPEUTIC EXPERIENCE

In my clinical practice, clients often come to me for help with infidelity recovery, whether it's the partner who betrayed looking for guidance on how to manage the crisis they've caused, or couples hoping to navigate the painful journey together. One thing is always clear: everyone involved is deeply hurt, scared, confused, and profoundly vulnerable. Both the betrayed and betraying partners are struggling with how to move forward, and my role is to create a bridge where safety can start to be felt for both partners. They need a space where they can explore their feelings, express their fears, and begin the difficult process of healing with great self-reflection.

Many of the men who come to me are either in the height of crisis after initial discovery, or they've tried various approaches and still haven't seen meaningful progress. Often, they've worked with other therapists who are not trained in the nuances of infidelity recovery, tried online programs, participated in 12-step programs, or sought help through pastoral counseling. Any of these approaches are meaningful if they bring the insight needed for moving ahead. However, when the situation hasn't improved, the men often begin their work with me dejected, untrusting, and hopeless. They're feeling overwhelmed and frustrated, unsure of how to fix the damage they've caused or how to manage the intense emotions that come erratically. By the time they reach me, they're looking for a fresh perspective, hoping that something will finally help them break through the pain and confusion.

When I first meet with these men, it is clear that their struggle is deeply rooted in hegemonic masculinity—referring to the theory I discussed in Chapter 2 that sees men as conditioned to suppress vulnerability, maintain emotional control, and prioritize strength and grounding. These societal expectations can intensify their internal conflict. That's because the crisis they face isn't just about the betrayal—it's about the way they've been taught to handle (or avoid) emotional pain. This emotional pain may have started long before the acts of infidelity. Many men feel unprepared to navigate the guilt, shame, and fear that accompany infidelity because it conflicts with the idea of being in control or being a good guy. They may resist seeking help, believing they should handle the situation on their own, or struggle with how to express their emotions in a way that is aligned with their sense of masculinity. My role is to help them challenge these norms, providing a space where they can explore vulnerability without feeling like it diminishes their strength or identity.

This process is also helpfully understood through the lens of social exchange theory, also discussed in Chapter 2, as the men have to navigate the costs and benefits of this work. In the wake of infidelity, both partners begin to reevaluate the costs of the betrayal against the potential benefits of staying together and rebuilding. Men who have betrayed their partners often feel an imbalance in this exchange—they worry that they no longer offer any benefits to the relationship, that the cost of their betrayal is too great to overcome, and they find themselves in a "one-down" position that challenges their sense of masculinity. For the relationship to heal, both partners must work to renegotiate the terms of their emotional exchange which is challenging because trust has been broken. The men must challenge their own vulnerability and fear and believe there is a value in developing transparency, emotional investment, and a willingness to give and receive in ways that were not part of the old relationship dynamic.

CLINICAL RESEARCH INTO MEN'S EXPERIENCE WITH THERAPY

In my efforts to better understand how men navigate the challenging path of infidelity recovery, I developed a national study focused on men who have sought treatment. (I've referred to this study in several parts of the book and quoted from it in Chapter 3.) In my study, I wanted to dive deeper into these men's experiences to uncover what approaches were truly effective and where the gaps were. Whether it was therapy, online programs, support groups, or pastoral counseling, I was curious to see what worked in helping these men move forward and what left them feeling stuck. This study allowed me to gather insights directly from those who had lived through the process, providing valuable information on how to improve treatment for men in similar situations.

This study had a strong focus on disenfranchised grief (explored in depth in Chapter 4) and how it shows up during the infidelity recovery process. Focusing on disenfranchised grief in therapy is crucial for helping men overcome infidelity, not only for their own benefit but also for the healing of their relationships and partners. Disenfranchised grief refers to the unacknowledged or invalidated emotions that men often experience when they are seen primarily as the betrayer in a relationship, with little attention given to their own emotional pain. When men feel unable to express their remorse, shame, or internal struggles because they believe their grief doesn't deserve recognition, they are left with unresolved emotions that can undermine their personal healing. Addressing these emotions allows men to process their guilt, gain insight into their behavior, and grow emotionally, which is necessary for genuine personal recovery and transformation. By giving voice to their grief, therapists can help men reclaim their sense of self-worth and move forward with a clearer understanding of how they can contribute positively to their relationship's repair.

In terms of relationship healing, acknowledging men's disenfranchised grief helps to rebuild trust and emotional intimacy with their partners. When the betraying partner is supported in addressing their own emotional wounds, they are more capable of being present for their partner's pain and helping to repair the damage caused by infidelity. This reciprocal healing process fosters a healthier, more balanced dynamic in which both partners can work together to rebuild their relationship. Without this focus the relationship risks remaining imbalanced, where the man may feel excluded from the healing process, leading to resentment or disengagement. By addressing their grief, men become more empathetic and emotionally available, which not only aids their personal growth but also supports their partner in feeling heard and validated, thus laying the foundation for a stronger, more resilient relationship.

To really understand how disenfranchised grief plays out in therapy, I first needed to know where men were turning for help and how they experienced those options. Men are often hesitant to seek mental health support because of stigma, and when they do, they may be dealing with the weight of social expectations around masculinity. For some, this means struggling to open up or feeling judged if they express vulnerability. Knowing what kind of support these men sought, and how their therapists were equipped to handle the grief and complexity of infidelity, was essential to understand how well—or poorly—they could process what they were going through.

Interestingly, many of the men I spoke with couldn't clearly identify their therapist's specific training or specialization. Some thought the therapist was knowledgeable about infidelity or addiction, but when asked for more details, they couldn't say for sure. Online support groups were a bit different—the men knew the facilitators were fellow survivors and spoke from personal experience, which, in some cases, made them feel more understood, even if they didn't have clinical credentials. Most of the men had tried a mix of individual therapy and couples therapy, whether it was ongoing sessions with a couples therapist, an intensive program like Affair Recovery, or even having their spouse join them in sessions with their individual therapist. But not everyone had this experience—like Charles, who said, "We didn't. I offered, and she said, 'No, you take care of what you need to take care of.'" It was a common thread. Several other men felt it was solely their job to repair the damage, leaving the men feeling alone in the process.

Men's Negative Experiences

Inconsistent involvement in couples work often added to the men's frustration. Michael, for example, wanted more regular sessions so he could feel united with his wife, but he said, "Sometimes my wife comes, sometimes she doesn't based on how she is feeling. It is up to her." This left him feeling disconnected and defeated. When partners would decide to attend sessions, it often turned into an opportunity for venting rather than skill-building or healing. Luke shared, "Couples therapy … it's intermittent … feels like a complaint session about all the things I've done." Without consistency, these men felt they never got the chance to share their own experience and pain. It's a clear link to disenfranchised grief—these men were grieving their own losses but felt unsupported and lacked a space to process their pain with their spouses.

The types of support varied with many trying to combine different options, trying to find something that fit. Most of the men in the study stated they felt they were working on recovery "full-time," as Frank put it, and were overwhelmed by the conflicting messages. It became clear that no matter the type of intervention, the relationship with the therapist or facilitator was critical. The way these men connected (or didn't) with their clinician shaped their ability to reflect on their own infidelity.

Negative experiences with therapists made all the men in my study decide to switch to a different individual therapist. But when it came to couples therapy, if their partner was happy, the men felt stuck, even if they weren't getting what they needed. Frank summed it up perfectly: "The reason it's working for me is because she is not leaving me. But if you ask me if his approach is good? The only reason I'm liking it is because the outcome that she's not leaving." For many, it wasn't until their partners were also dissatisfied that a change in couples therapy approach was even considered.

Although men often hold privilege and power socially, they also face higher rates of mental issues, behavioral challenges, and difficulties in maintaining quality intimate relationships. This is particularly relevant when it comes to infidelity recovery, as men are generally less likely to seek out supportive mental health services. And, when they do seek help, it's crucial clinicians understand how to work effectively with men. In couples therapy, many men struggle because the way they've been socialized creates a tension between seeking help and expressing vulnerability, especially in front of a partner who is hurt by their actions. It's essential for a counselor to create a space where men feel safe to express their fears and explore accountability without feeling diminished. When therapy fails to do this, men often struggle to connect their behavior to the underlying emotional experiences, making it harder for them to repair their relationship.

Many men I've worked with shared their negative therapy experiences that left them feeling punished or reduced, rather than supported. They described feeling as though they were being pushed through therapy without understanding why certain actions were expected of them or feeling that the couples therapy was unfairly skewed toward their partner. Alan noted, "I felt like when we met with her, she focused mostly on my wife, where her head was, how she was processing." Similarly, Frank expressed, "My emotions should be protected. My emotions should be recognized. I don't think he does a good job on that front." These moments left them feeling unsupported, often increasing feelings of guilt, shame, or frustration. Some men, like Harry, felt outright attacked in sessions: "The therapist just basically started plowing me down ... kind of laying into me kind of hard." When therapy didn't feel balanced or helpful, many men walked away disillusioned, feeling as though they had no place in the process.

These negative experiences in therapy often made things worse at home. Without the neutral guidance they needed to help navigate tough emotions, the relationship grew more hostile and the path to healing became even more unclear. Alan spoke about feeling belittled by the therapist, saying, "I welcomed it. I already knew she wasn't telling me anything I didn't already know," suggesting he accepted it because he didn't feel he deserved any better. For many, ineffective therapy became a source of deeper conflict. Harry's story reflects this, as he described the escalation of violence at home after failed therapy: "She completely lost it, I completely lost it.... I ended up getting hit." These men clearly linked their disappointing therapy experiences to why their marriages didn't improve as they had hoped, reinforcing the importance of finding the right therapeutic support.

The stories shared by these men further highlight the lack of support and encouragement that many men face when seeking mental and emotional help. In therapeutic settings, especially in a couples context, men are often socialized to avoid advocating for themselves and resort to shutting down or becoming defensive, especially when there is a two-to-one dynamic at play. As I said in Chapter 3, I advocate that the client in the room should be the relationship and not one partner over another. It is not helpful to the relationship if either partner is working to get the therapist "on their side." Infidelity happened because the dynamic in the relationship was challenged and now that discovery or disclosure has happened, both partners must face the often painful and confusing reality of the new dynamic with a sense of security that the therapist is there to help them navigate it safely. However, much of the literature on infidelity focuses on the pain and injury of the betrayed partner. While some authors do advocate for a less reactive approach, it's clear that the feelings and experiences of the men themselves often go unnoticed or undervalued. Infidelity recovery is deeply challenged if the man is not able to resolve what brought him into infidelity in the first place.

Going back to hegemonic masculinity theory as discussed in Chapter 2, it becomes evident that masculinity is shaped by complex power dynamics and contradictions that influence how men perceive their available options. In the aftermath of infidelity, these men grappled with conflicting desires; on one hand, they wanted to address their own needs, while on the other, they felt compelled to stabilize and fix their partner's emotional state after their actions had caused upheaval in the relationship. Many described couples therapy as primarily for their partner's healing, viewing participation as a way to atone for their mistakes. Brian put it succinctly: "Emotionally, I am still that insecure person that wants to see gratification and wants to feel that we're making progress, but...." Isaac echoed this sentiment, sharing that he feared expressing his needs could lead to deeper conflict. "I perceive that speaking my needs can absolutely lead to conflict if the response I get is, 'Well, maybe we're just not suited for each other.'" In these scenarios, the men often found themselves trapped in a fundamental gap, unsure of how to bridge it.

This raises several critical points worth considering. As the men pointed out, therapy often seemed centered on their partner's needs, leaving little room for them to focus on their own healing, pain, and growth or evolution. This dynamic reflects a societal conditioning that suggests prioritizing one's own mental and emotional health isn't valid. Moreover, it invites the question of who the "identified client" is within the therapy. If the focus is only on one partner, the approach might miss vital aspects of the relationship as a whole. Conversely, if the relationship itself is treated as the identified client, the clinician is not addressing the union if one of the partners is not engaged. It's crucial for clinicians to assess why the man is in therapy, both for his own well-being and the future of the relationship, creating a space that acknowledges and validates his experiences.

A clear example of how these struggles manifest can be seen in the examples of men who reported little to no sexual engagement with their partners post-infidelity. Charles summed up his experience, "She and I still have not had sex…. It's going on close to four years, so that need has not been met…. I weigh all my needs against each other and make judgments. That's just simply a need I'm not gonna have met." Frank shared a similar story: "We haven't had sex yet. It can't happen. I'm hoping it happens soon … but it's up to her to decide, and I just have to wait." When asked if they discussed their sexual concerns in therapy, these men stated that while it was important to them, it wasn't a focus in treatment and the therapist didn't identify it as a concern. Isaac expressed frustration when he tried to bring it up with his therapist: "He just kind of sidestepped it…. I don't think he really wanted to focus on it." These men were left grappling with how to hold onto their masculine identity while humbly seeking forgiveness and waiting for their partner's emotional readiness—without any meaningful role models or direction for positive forward movement. This dynamic reflects the internal contradictions of hegemonic masculinity, contributing to the emotional struggles many of these men described later in the study. Their grief, stemming from a lack of sexual connection, was disenfranchised by therapists who avoided engaging their feelings of loss and need for intimacy. Clinicians must be able to acknowledge and address men's need for sexual healing, even if their partner isn't ready to re-engage in physical intimacy. The key is to address the issue and explore it either in individual or couples therapy.

When men reported negative experiences in therapy, they described feelings of being misunderstood, judged, or diminished. Many men who left therapy or struggled to stay with a therapist mentioned that the clinician didn't connect with them, remained silent and expected them to talk, or immediately focused on their mistakes without first building a rapport. George, who tried several therapists, shared his frustration: "For a person like me, or anyone who cheats, it can't be a therapist that sits and says, 'Tell me how that makes you feel.' It has to be forced. You're in so much denial and so self-deflective that type of therapist just doesn't work." Most men who felt disconnected from their therapists couldn't even remember their names. On the other hand, several men who attended 12-step programs had mixed experiences. While John was a strong advocate, others, especially those referred to Sex and Love Addicts Anonymous (SLAA), expressed negative feelings due to the stigma attached to the program. Evan explained,

"If you dare say you are a sex addict, that means I'm a pedophile, that I'm just a monster." This added shame made participation in SLAA more difficult than other programs like Alcoholics Anonymous or Narcotics Anonymous. Many men felt the meetings lacked meaningful support, understanding, or continuity. Evan recalled arriving at a meeting and seeing "Phones on top of garbage cans ... guys letting their wives know they're at a meeting." The disconnection, lack of engagement, and absence of guidance left many men feeling even more isolated in their recovery journey.

Hegemonic masculinity and its associated expectations for performance are deeply embedded in men's self-concept, creating a gender role strain that can exacerbate addiction, stunt personal growth, and impact the therapeutic process. Addictive behaviors, such as alcohol or substance abuse, can amplify a man's sense of self in destructive ways, allowing him to exploit his privilege while acting out. Yet, when it comes to seeking help, these same masculine ideals increase self-stigma, making the recovery process more difficult. Without proper guidance and a structured intervention, this hegemonic masculinity leads to further suffering, compounding feelings of shame and guilt, especially in the aftermath of infidelity.

MEN'S POSITIVE EXPERIENCES

In contrast, when men reported positive therapeutic experiences, they were able to take greater ownership of their repair work and feel the direct benefits of their emotional investment. These men identified key elements like feeling heard without judgment, experiencing a decrease in isolation, and releasing negative thoughts and feelings. Ken described his experience: "It was much more a forward-looking kind of approach. It wasn't 'let's move on,' but a lot of it was building me up." Evan similarly shared: "The therapist made me feel like I was not a monster." For many, this was the first and only place they felt a sense of agency after the disclosure or discovery of infidelity.

This sense of agency became particularly crucial for men whose infidelity became public knowledge, resulting in widespread judgment and ridicule. Evan, for example, spoke about the public shaming he endured: "Everybody knew. The only thing she didn't do was get a billboard. I work in a small town, so it didn't take long for it to get around, especially at the rate she was advertising and embellishing it. So the stigma of being a cheater...." In these cases, clinicians became lifelines, offering men a safe space to process their feelings without being vilified.

Ken and Evan's stories are clear examples of how clinicians can play an essential role in facilitating a man's healing and reshaping his identity. Ken's therapist, for instance, didn't focus solely on the details of the infidelity but helped him to reconceptualize himself, allowing for personal growth. This shift in focus—from shame and guilt to self-awareness and agency—enabled Ken to see himself in a new light. For Evan, whose life had become the subject of public judgment, his therapist provided a counter-narrative. The clinician helped him to look at his own experiences without being overwhelmed by the need to maintain a stoic façade. Instead of being consumed by the public's perception of him, Evan was empowered to build his own narrative, reclaiming his sense of self beyond the infidelity.

These positive experiences highlight how effective clinical intervention can address the disenfranchised grief men face in the aftermath of infidelity. By engaging with the client's experience and understanding the unique challenges he faces—both internally and externally—clinicians can help men navigate their emotional turmoil and rebuild their sense of identity in healthier, more constructive ways.

The men in the study identified several key areas where they experienced positive outcomes due to a meaningful connection with their therapist. These included making healthier choices, developing better communication skills, improving their sex life with their partner, feeling supported and heard, creating new relationship structures, gaining personal insights, and fostering a greater sense of self. Communication skills in particular were the most frequently reported area of improvement, helping the men manage the intense emotional responses of their partners and establish boundaries in conversations. Nate, for example, described how therapy helped him create structured conversations: "It gets to a point where the conversation gets intense, and I need to pull back.... We've got ways where we've started using tools in the discussion about this and for 45 minutes we're gonna talk, and then after 45 minutes we're gonna see where we are, and if you need to take a break, we'll take a break."

The emphasis on healthy communication allowed men to become active listeners and reflect back on new understandings, leading to more meaningful conversations and emotional exchanges. About half the men also reported their sex life had improved, attributing the progress directly to their therapeutic work. For example, Evan described his sexual relationship as "way better" post-infidelity therapy, noting the intimacy had evolved into a more connected experience. George also reported improvement, although he expressed a desire for his wife to initiate sex more often: "Far more than we used to … unfortunately, she doesn't initiate it. I have to." Even Michael noted, "Yeah…. There's been a big change. It is actually happening and fun now."

These improvements revealed that therapists who recognized the men's inability to express their pain or desires were instrumental in facilitating healing. By creating treatment plans that supported self-advocacy, helped them explore their hesitancies, and strengthened their distress tolerance, the therapists counteracted the disenfranchised grief that previously silenced the men. Through these efforts, many of the men learned to identify and express their needs, developing the confidence to speak their truth in ways that contributed to both their individual healing and the healing of their relationships.

Overall, the men who formed a strong connection with their therapist reported significant positive changes in how they viewed themselves and their relationships. They developed new ways of being in relationships, experienced growth in self-concept, and held onto hope for their future. George's experience, in particular, illustrates the life-changing impact of personalized therapeutic care. Prior to the discovery of his infidelity, George had been suicidal. He reflected on his progress: "I told my wife, 'If you didn't find out, you wouldn't have a husband, and the kids wouldn't have a father…. I owe my life to my wife…. I owe my confidence to myself…. You can't tiptoe around recovery work … therapy taught me that. Honestly … it's helped me 95% of where I am at." George credited his therapist with focusing on the grief and pain he hadn't been able to articulate prior to treatment. It was the personalized, tailored approach—not a generic or programmatic one—that helped him recognize the importance of his own experience.

However, not all stories were marked by consistent success. Harry, who formed a strong bond with his therapist, struggled to stay focused due to his substance use and mental health challenges. Despite his connection to therapy, Harry's inconsistent attendance led to his therapist ending treatment. Reflecting on the process, Harry shared, "I actually entered therapy…. I loved it; I ended up loving therapy…. I was actually shocked how almost everything there was something we were working on … by the time we got toward the end of working on it, I answered myself.… I got fired for missing too many appointments." Despite the challenges, Harry's therapist helped him find his own voice, offering him validation and empowering him to speak for himself for the first time. Sadly, Harry's chaotic life circumstances hindered his ability to fully engage in consistent therapeutic work, demonstrating the importance of a stable environment for the therapy to have its intended long-term impact.

Three of the men—Alan, Evan, and Isaac—shared how their therapists helped them not only tell their stories but also reflect on the personal growth they experienced through therapy. Now, they even speak in groups like Affair Recovery, supporting other men who are struggling with infidelity. Their therapists focused on helping them feel supported, naming their emotions, and developing the courage to speak openly about their experiences. As a result, these men reported their partners have noticed the changes they've made and appreciate the ownership they've taken. Of course, their partners still have moments of anger or jealousy. As Alan mentioned, his wife felt "mostly anger, disbelief, and shock." Isaac's wife also expressed jealousy, saying, "You did this with the affair partner, but you can't or won't do that with me?" The difference now, however, is that the men handle these emotional outbursts with more care, focusing on reconnecting with their partners rather than just trying to stabilize or minimize the situation.

The men also opened up about how the public exposure of the infidelity impacted their sense of self, particularly in terms of authority and agency within their relationships and family dynamics. Many described how their partner's rage led to a very public airing of their actions, including to family, friends, and even on social media. This public shaming left some of them feeling like they had nowhere to escape the pain. Through therapy, though, they were able to regain a sense of self. Evan, for instance, talked about how everyone in his town and workplace knew every detail of his affair. Isaac, on the other hand, spoke about how shame caused him to withdraw from social circles, even church. But therapy shifted the focus from just the infidelity to a deeper exploration of their identity and how they connected to their stories. The men who developed strong therapeutic relationships spoke about the future with hope, emphasizing personal growth. Alan said, "If you keep working, you never give up hope." Others, like Brian and Harry, struggled with connecting to therapists and remained stuck in the cycles of guilt and shame. These cases highlight how important it is for therapists to focus on helping men rebuild their sense of self, especially after the emotional damage of public shaming. When therapists can do this, the healing process becomes more meaningful and long-lasting.

From a hegemonic masculinity perspective, men often face significant challenges when responding to emotional injuries or situations that disrupt their sense of identity and authority. The ability to create a safe and nurturing space in therapy relies heavily on a clinician's ability to approach men with a gender-sensitive lens. Hegemonic masculinity should not be thought of as entirely about emotional detachment and strong independence. In reality, men struggle emotionally when their masculinity is in crisis. This is why therapists must be culturally aware, understanding the central role masculinity plays in shaping a man's identity. Helping a man shift his behavior, develop new communication skills, and build healthier relationships requires a deep comprehension of how tightly masculinity is intertwined with his sense of self. For men in therapy, once they felt the pressure of these expectations releasing, they found themselves able to access emotions and create new identities they hadn't realized were possible before.

Harry, for instance, described how his normally stoic demeanor would crack during sessions when he reflected on the possibility of losing his wife. He shared, "Anything that had to do with losing my wife, I would just shut down. I would start crying. I actually cried almost every time we talked about her." Luke had a similar experience with his therapist, who empowered him to prioritize his own recovery and self-discovery. His therapist made it clear that their time together was for Luke's personal growth, telling him, "This is for you. This is our time to work together for you." These men learned that, contrary to societal pressures, being vulnerable and working on their authentic selves was a path to healing, not a sign of weakness.

Those men who formed meaningful connections with their therapists often likened their recovery to reclaiming their sense of masculinity, with their counselors helping them to view themselves as brave warriors needing guidance rather than failures. The therapists approached the infidelity with a nonjudgmental stance, allowing the men to take ownership without shame. Oscar's story was a great example of this. In therapy, he realized he couldn't "fix" his wife's pain, saying, "I can't control whether she understands.... It may just take time for her to accept." Ken, who faced a heart surgery immediately after the discovery of his infidelity, shared how his therapist helped him reflect on who he wanted to be during his recovery. This new awareness helped him realize, "That's not who I am ... but I also want to make sure I can support her because she deserves whatever feelings she has." Through their therapeutic journeys, these men found healing not just for themselves but for their relationships, rebuilding trust and connection with their partners through shared commitment.

Overall, the men's positive experiences with therapy underscore the power of meaningful, personalized clinical interventions. When therapists were able to connect deeply with their male clients, offering validation and tools for self-advocacy, the men felt empowered to navigate their healing with greater confidence, communication skills, and emotional resilience.

THERAPEUTIC INTERCONNECTIONS

The third major area of focus regarding therapeutic connection centered on the alignment and coordination between different treatment processes. When a man is seeing both an individual therapist and a couples therapist, or engaging in external support groups or 12-step programs, the integration of these services becomes critical to his overall therapeutic experience. If these resources are aligned—meaning the messages, strategies, and goals from each provider are consistent— it can significantly enhance the man's ability to make holistic progress. However, when there's a disconnect between these services, it can create confusion, frustration, or even stall his recovery.

The ease with which men can access and engage in these services often depends on how well their providers communicate with each other. Whether it's basic communication between individual and couples therapists, coordinated planning of treatment, or true collaboration, the effectiveness of therapy improves when the care team is on the same page. For men already facing challenges with vulnerability and seeking help, the seamless coordination of care becomes a lifeline.

The men who reported the most positive therapeutic experiences highlighted the importance of this alignment. When their therapists and facilitators communicated and shared consistent messages, the men felt a great sense of fairness and support. They developed strong communication skills, and crucially, began to see themselves as more than their actions. For example, many men talked about feeling a deeper ownership of their recovery, experiencing a release from shame, and gaining a renewed sense of self. The message that "You are more than your mistakes" resonated more deeply when they heard it reinforced by multiple professionals, leading them to internalize it as truth.

Oscar's experience exemplifies this. He initially felt overwhelmed and incapable of change, thinking of himself as an "extreme deviant" beyond help. But when his individual therapist and his couples therapist both communicated the same message—that he wasn't uniquely flawed and could move forward with the right support—he started to believe it. "I think we are fortunate that we really found someone in these two therapists who've made the commitment to us as well," Oscar said, emphasizing the power of coordinated care. This speaks to a key aspect of hegemonic masculinity: men are often shaped by their social environments, and when individuals they perceive as having authority (like therapists) offer them a path to regain their masculine identity through new behaviors, they are more likely to embrace it.

By creating a unified sense of accountability, the coordination of therapeutic messages allowed these men to feel supported and validated. This alignment of treatment processes gave them the tools to better communicate with their partners, restore their sense of self-worth, and take ownership of their actions, all while integrating these changes into their daily lives. It is clear that the impact of therapy is magnified when the messages are consistent, coordinated, and delivered by multiple trusted voices.

However, when there is a misalignment between therapists, many men find themselves gravitating toward the messages that align with their existing narratives, or worse, disengaging from the therapeutic process altogether. Frank's experience is a prime example of how a lack of coordination between therapists can derail recovery. His individual therapist was guiding him through a process of reconciliation by fostering better communication, self-awareness, and restructuring his relationships. Meanwhile, his couples therapist, who refused to coordinate with his individual therapist, was biased toward the wife's perspective. Since Franks's wife had made his infidelity public, the couples therapist instructed him to join a 12-step program, apologize individually to every member of his wife's family and close friends, and take the MMPI (Minnesota Multiphasic Personality Inventory) to assess his mental health. Every week, Frank was required to report his progress in front of his wife and the couples therapist, creating a dynamic that felt punitive.

Frank was caught between two therapists with conflicting approaches. His individual therapist disagreed with the couples therapist's recommendation for Frank to apologize to so many people, given that the recovery was with his wife. Forcing Frank to apologize to so many people only served to further shame him and ensure the public nature of his pain remained public. Additionally, the individual therapist was unsupportive of taking the MMPI, believing that labeling Frank with a mental health diagnosis would not contribute positively to his recovery. Frank expressed his confusion: "One of the actions was for me to take an MMPI test to see if I'm crazy or not. Which, okay, it costs a lot, and my individual therapist is totally against it because he thinks having a label on myself won't help me in any way." This conflict between therapists, who failed to coordinate their treatment plans, left Frank feeling lost and unsupported. It also highlights the challenge men face when they are forced to navigate conflicting messages within their treatment.

For many men, therapeutic settings where they receive negative or unhelpful messages become spaces to merely endure while they wait to meet with a more supportive clinician. Alan shared how one therapist simply reinforced a message he already knew: "She just listened and nodded. And I think she wanted to reinforce the fact that this was my decision.... Our group therapist has really helped me in many parts of my life, not just my relationship." In contrast, John expressed his frustration with a clinician who placed the burden of responsibility solely on him. "It felt like everything was my fault and that I needed to fix everything ... and, by the way, you don't seem to have the tools to fix it, and I'm not equipped to help you develop those tools. It was very one-sided."

These negative experiences not only drained the men emotionally but also undid the progress they were making with the supportive therapists. Much of the time spent with positive clinicians was dedicated to undoing the damage caused by the negative ones. The men felt that their emotions weren't recognized or protected in the less supportive therapeutic spaces, which ultimately led some of them to disengage from treatment. Frank's words capture this sense of exhaustion: "I don't know how long I can keep it up, to be honest." When men receive conflicting or harmful messages from their care team, it creates a sense of futility that threatens their willingness to continue their recovery journey.

These stories underscore the importance of coordinated care and alignment among treatment providers. When clinicians work together, men feel supported, validated, and empowered to change. But when there's a disconnect, the emotional toll can be overwhelming, leading to feelings of isolation and hopelessness.

The second most common form of misalignment reported by the men came from their experiences with 12-step programs. While 12-step programs can be deeply impactful and meaningful, using them for infidelity recovery can be confusing and misaligned. Out of the group of men who attended some form of 12-step program, only John found it to be deeply meaningful and aligned with his other treatment modalities. The remaining men in my study, like Harry and Frank, participated in these programs primarily because they were required to as part of their couples therapy. For Evan and Ken, however, the programs were not particularly impactful, as they felt a disconnect between what they were told the mission of the intervention was and how other participants were held accountable.

Ken and Evan expressed frustration with the lack of engagement they observed from others in the program. They noted that many partic-ipants seemed to be going through the motions, attending meetings simply to meet the expectations of their therapists or partners without genuinely engaging in the recovery process. Evan shared a particularly disheartening example of how some men "gamed the system" by leaving their phones on a rack at the meeting location, so their partners—who were tracking them via phone locator—could see they were present. Meanwhile, these men would leave the meeting without participating.

This behavior led to a deep sense of disappointment for Ken and Evan. Because hegemonic masculinity is often comparative, with men using one another as benchmarks for their own standing, the low level of commitment displayed by other participants caused them to ques-tion the value of 12-step programs. Instead of striving for personal growth, the men reported lowering their expectations of what could be achieved in these meetings.

Their language around this misalignment conveyed feelings of disillusionment and unfairness. The men had entered the 12-step program with the hope of becoming better, yet they found themselves in environments where other participants were only going through the motions, leaving them feeling unsupported and frustrated by the forced engagement. This left them questioning the overall effectiveness of the intervention.

What becomes clear from the men in my study is that the process of infidelity recovery is complex and nuanced. Clinicians working in individual or couple therapy must create spaces where these men can learn complex new skills that allow for self-evaluation. This self-evaluation can then support the man's ability to partner in healthy ways promoting communication, vulnerability, self-awareness, and honesty. I think of this as a three-legged stool with each leg (the man, his partner, and the clinicians working with them) doing their part to support the creation of a new and stable structure that can hold the relationship. If just one of those legs is not stable and strong, the stool falls.

Chapter

7

▼

Understanding the Man's Emotional Experience in Infidelity Recovery

For men who have committed infidelity, the therapeutic work often involves understanding how the infidelity reflects the larger patterns in the relationship and focusing on rebuilding emotional intimacy. Addressing both personal accountability and the relationship's dynamics is key. It's vital to explore what was broken within the relationship that led to the betrayal, and how both partners can work together to repair the rupture. Recognizing the relational context of the infidelity helps move beyond shame and punishment, creating space for deeper healing and growth.

It can be deeply challenging for the betrayed partner to accept that the relationship wasn't ideal or that there were dynamics both partners were responsible for. The initial shock and pain of the betrayal often make it hard to look beyond the immediate hurt and into the larger context of the relationship. Understandably, many betrayed partners feel that their partner's choice to cheat is the sole issue, and it can seem invalidating to suggest that relational dynamics played a role. When a partner says, "Yeah, but I didn't cheat!" it highlights a very real pain— they were not the ones who crossed the boundary. This response is valid and meaningful, as the hurt caused by infidelity is significant and must be acknowledged before deeper healing can occur.

However, while the betrayed partner's pain is absolutely real, focusing only on the act of cheating can sometimes obscure the broader issues in the relationship that contributed to the breakdown. Emotional coping skills vary widely, and as discussed in Chapter 2 on hegemonic masculinity and social exchange theories, men often face different challenges in processing their emotions. These theories explain that societal norms and expectations can make it difficult for men to express vulnerability or address dissatisfaction in healthy ways. Instead, they may turn to infidelity as a misguided form of emotional escape. This doesn't excuse the behavior, but it does provide a framework for understanding how the relationship may have influenced their choices.

The most challenging part of the Crisis phase I talked about in "The Arc of Infidelity Recovery" chapter is finding a balance between helping the man fully own what he did and supporting the partner in recognizing that the infidelity didn't happen in a vacuum. This requires careful navigation. The betrayed partner needs validation for their pain, but it's also essential for both partners to explore the relational dynamics that allowed the emotional distance or dissatisfaction to grow. This work involves helping the man develop emotional awareness and accountability while supporting the betrayed partner in understanding that while they didn't cheat, there may have been underlying issues that contributed to the disconnect. Both individuals need space to process their own emotions, but eventually, the couple must come together to address the relationship as a whole.

Referring back to the work of Zapien and others discussed in "The Basics of Infidelity" chapter, it's essential to explore the precedents that often lead to infidelity. Zapien's research highlights that infidelity rarely occurs in a vacuum—there are usually patterns and dynamics within the relationship that create fertile ground for betrayal. These precedents may include emotional disconnection, unresolved conflicts, or unmet needs that neither partner has yet fully addressed. For the man, this could mean avoiding difficult conversations or using external validation as a way to cope with feelings of inadequacy or dissatisfaction. For the betrayed partner, it might include unintentionally reinforcing those patterns by not recognizing or addressing the underlying issues in time. By identifying these precedents, both partners can gain a clearer understanding of the broader relationship dynamics that contributed to the infidelity.

Again, however, identifying these patterns is not about excusing the choices made during the affair, which were deeply hurtful and damaging. Instead, it's about helping both partners see the full scope of what was happening in the relationship before the betrayal. This process is key to moving forward because it shifts the focus from simply punishing the man for his actions to understanding how the relationship, as a whole, became unsteady. When both partners can see the broader dynamics, they're better equipped to rebuild a foundation of trust and intimacy. It opens up space for healing, not just from the specific acts of infidelity but from the emotional wounds and relational disconnect that existed long before. This understanding doesn't minimize the man's responsibility, but it helps both partners approach the process of repair with more insight and compassion.

Learning from the Man's Experience During the Affair

The men I have worked with in therapy often share that there were many aspects of their affair that felt exciting and intriguing. For some, the affair brought a sense of newness and adventure—an escape from the routine of their daily lives or relationships. Many describe feeling an obsessive pull toward the affair, with the secrecy and heightened emotions adding to the allure. In those moments, they might have felt desired, powerful, or energized in ways that had been missing from their primary relationship. The affair can be seen as a temporary reprieve from the emotional challenges they were facing, providing a sense of immediate gratification.

However, these men also talk about the less glamorous side of their experiences—feelings of disconnection, isolation, and even fear. Despite the initial thrill, many report a growing sense of discomfort as the affair progressed. They often felt emotionally split, struggling to maintain the façade of normalcy in their primary relationship while living a double life. This disconnection led to isolation, as they couldn't confide in anyone about the emotional toll the affair was taking on them. Fear became a constant companion, whether it was the fear of being discovered or the anxiety of how their choices would impact their loved ones. These feelings were often more pervasive than the excitement, making the affair a deeply conflicted experience that left them emotionally exhausted and confused.

When the fear of discovery wasn't consuming them, many men I've worked with became highly adept at compartmentalizing their affairs. They developed the ability to mentally separate the affair from their everyday life, allowing them to function in both worlds without fully confronting the emotional conflict this dual existence created. In therapy, they often describe how the affair felt like a separate reality— almost like a video game that they could pick up and play when they wanted, then put down when it wasn't convenient. This mental separation allowed them to return to their "real" lives with a sense of normalcy, continuing to engage with their partner, family, and work while pushing aside the emotional complexity of their secret relationship.

However, the affair always played in the background, even when they weren't actively engaging in it. Compartmentalization provided an escape, but it also enabled them to maintain the illusion that they could manage both worlds without consequence. The ability to step into the affair and then back into their daily life created a parallel experience that allowed them to avoid fully addressing the emotional impact of their actions. This mental distancing often gave them a false sense of control, as if they could keep their "real life" intact while indulging in escapist behaviors that fulfilled unmet emotional needs. Yet, over time, the strain of living these parallel lives became increasingly difficult, as the boundaries between the compartments began to blur, leading to heightened anxiety, guilt, and emotional conflict.

As an affair progressed, many men began to feel emotionally exhausted and worn down by the constant effort it took to maintain the duality of their lives. They often reported that to keep the affair alive, they had to say things that would keep their affair partner emotionally invested. Intimate statements about love, desire, and future possibilities become part of the script they felt compelled to follow. While some of these statements may have felt genuine in the moment, they were more often part of the "affair script"—a series of phrases and actions that allow the man to sustain the fantasy and the compartmentalization between his affair and real life. This emotional exertion became draining, as it required constant upkeep to keep the façade going, even when the excitement of the affair had faded.

Many men in therapy have shared that the type of intimacy expressed in the affair was something they felt was missing in their primary relationship, which contributed to their desire to engage in the affair in the first place. However, as so many men discuss in the study I conducted (discussed in Chapters 3 and 6), and as they discuss in treatment, this intimacy is often superficial, driven more by the affair's structure than by a deep emotional connection. For example, when asked why he told his affair partner that he loved her, Joe, a client in one of our sessions, responded, "She said it to me. She kept telling me how hot I was ... about all the things she wanted to do to me ... and I just said it. It was expected, and it fit the story." In this way, the affair takes on a script-like quality, where the man feels the need to keep the affair partner emotionally hooked, even if it means saying things that aren't entirely genuine.

Over time, this script can become more of a burden than a thrill. The man might find himself constantly feeding the affair partner with affirmations and fantasies that keep the illusion alive, but these words and actions can start to feel hollow. Many men report feeling disconnected from the intimacy they once found exciting, as the affair became more about managing expectations and maintaining the dual life than experiencing genuine emotional connection. The emotional exhaustion grew, and the compartmentalization that once allowed the men to juggle both lives started to break down, leading to increasing feelings of guilt, dissatisfaction, and inner conflict.

For many men, the desire to end an affair can be overshadowed by the complexity of the situation they find themselves in. Initially, the affair may have provided excitement or an emotional escape, but over time, it often evolved into something far more difficult to manage. The secrecy, the emotional manipulation, and the pressure from the affair partner can make it nearly impossible for these men to find a clear way out. As Ben described in one session, "She kept threatening to tell my wife and my boss. I couldn't see how to end it, and the affair became more of a burden than I had bargained for." This fear of exposure traps men in a situation where they feel unable to end the affair without devastating consequences, leaving them feeling powerless.

The feeling of being "held hostage" by the affair partner is not uncommon. Many men feel that their affair partner wields a signifi-cant amount of power over their lives, especially when the affair partner threatens to reveal the relationship to the man's spouse or employer. Marc, another client, shared his experience, saying, "When I told her I wanted to end it and work on my marriage, she had a big reaction and told me that she would ruin me if I didn't keep seeing her." This fear can prevent men from taking the steps necessary to end the affair, even when they deeply want to repair their primary relationship. The emotional intensity and manipulation involved can leave them feeling trapped, unable to act on their desire to come clean and rebuild their marriage.

The consequences of these complicated dynamics often come to light in painful ways. In Marc's case, it wasn't until his affair partner's husband found out about the affair that the situation unraveled. "He called my wife," Marc explained, "and they got divorced. I am just thankful that my wife continues to let me stay in the house while we try to work it out." The aftermath of these revelations can be devastating, with multiple lives affected and the man left facing the wreckage of both his affair and his marriage. Even if the man's primary partner decides to stay and work on the relationship, the damage is significant, and the process of healing is long and difficult.

For many men, the end of an affair brings a complex mix of emotions. While there is often a deep sense of relief, particularly when the fear of exposure and the emotional strain of maintaining the affair are lifted, that relief is accompanied by the pain and agony in their primary relationship. Men frequently express in therapy how liberating it feels to no longer be living a double life, but this newfound freedom is hard to reconcile with the devastation they've caused. The challenge comes in navigating this dual experience—feeling personally relieved but simultaneously attending to their partner's profound hurt. This conflicting emotional state can be incredibly confusing for the man and expressing it to his partner is fraught with difficulty.

The relief that comes from escaping the binds of the affair often seems incongruent with the depth of betrayal the partner is experiencing. Many betrayed partners struggle to believe that the man genuinely wanted out of the affair, particularly if the affair only came to light because of discovery or exposure. This creates a disconnect where the man's desire to escape the affair isn't understood or validated. He may hear things like, "If you wanted out, why didn't you end it yourself?" or "You only stopped because you got caught." These statements, while understandable from the partner's perspective, can leave the man feeling even more misunderstood. His feelings of relief are real, but the inability to express them without causing further pain makes the situation even more complex.

As a result, many men in therapy report feeling trapped in their emotional experiences. They are free from the affair but still bound by the agony of trying to repair their primary relationship. The inability to talk openly about the relief they feel for fear of being judged or misunderstood can lead to feelings of isolation. They may find it difficult to validate their own emotions, especially when their partner is in so much pain. The challenge is in finding a balance—acknowledging both the relief that comes with the end of the affair and the responsibility for the hurt they've caused. Without a space to process these conflicting feelings, the man can feel lost, adding another layer of complexity to the already difficult journey of infidelity recovery.

When infidelity takes the form of a transactional encounter or a series of transactions, the same sense of relief that accompanies the end of a more emotionally involved affair can still be present. Many men, like Will, feel a release when their partner discovers their behavior. Will admitted in couples therapy, "If she didn't find out, I am not sure I would have stopped. It was like I knew I wanted to stop, but the pattern just kept going." In cases where the infidelity involves transactional experiences—whether it be with sex workers or casual, impersonal encounters—the man may feel trapped in a cycle of behavior that he knows is damaging but struggles to break on his own. The relief he feels once it's out in the open comes from no longer having to carry the burden of secrecy.

The transactional nature of this infidelity can sometimes make it harder for the man to understand his own actions. While he may not have been emotionally attached, the behavior often becomes a compulsive pattern—something that continues even though he recognizes its harm. Men in therapy frequently describe knowing their behavior is wrong but feeling powerless to change it. This confusion can lead to deep internal conflict: they don't feel the same emotional pull to the infidelity as in an affair, yet they are still caught up in a cycle that feels nearly impossible to break. The exposure, then, provides a kind of forced intervention, a disruption of the pattern that they may not have been able to achieve alone.

This sense of forced relief, however, is difficult to explain to a betrayed partner. The partner might struggle to understand how the man could continue with something he knew was wrong, and why he didn't stop sooner. For the man, though, the transactional nature of his actions means he may not have fully confronted the emotional or relational consequences until discovery occurred. As Will expressed, "At least now everything in the dark is in the light.... I can't hide from it anymore." While this can be a moment of clarity, it also brings confusion, guilt, and the challenge of explaining the disconnect between knowing a behavior is harmful and being unable to stop it.

REVISITING THE ARC OF INFIDELITY RECOVERY AS IT APPLIES IN THERAPY: CRISIS

The point of discovery or disclosure is often one of the most intense and emotionally charged moments in the journey of infidelity recovery. For the man who committed the infidelity, it marks the moment when the secrets he has carried, sometimes for months or years, are forced into the light. The initial shockwave that follows discovery can be overwhelming. This moment is filled with confusion and uncertainty, as the man grapples with the fallout of his actions and the fear of what will happen next. It's also the first time he may fully appreciate the depth of the consequences for his relationship and his life. Coming to therapy—individual and/or couples therapy—can often feel like a lifeline.

At the start of therapy, men who have committed infidelity are often in crisis mode. They come to therapy emotionally raw, and their immediate focus is on containing the damage, either trying to save the relationship or at least make sense of what just happened. In the initial stages, men often experience a range of emotions—fear of losing their partner, guilt over their actions, and, in some cases, relief that the secrecy has been lifted. Many report feeling like they're living in a state of chaos, unsure of how to begin rebuilding trust or addressing the pain they've caused. Therapy becomes a critical space where these overwhelming feelings can be processed and where the first steps toward healing can be taken. Often, just showing up for appointments feels like relief. In individual work, the client can express openly without immediate blowback based on what he says. In effective couples therapy, there is a third party to help mitigate the emotional turmoil that is being hurled his way.

One of the early challenges in therapy is helping men face the complexity of their own emotions. Many men express a desire to fix the situation quickly, wanting to move past the pain and discomfort as soon as possible. There is a deep desire to be able to say, "Hey, I get this ... I fucked up but I will never do it again ... I will be better!" However, infidelity recovery is not a quick or linear process. In therapy, men must learn to sit with their guilt and shame while also taking owner-ship of their actions. This is particularly difficult because, in the initial phases of therapy, the focus is often on identifying the betrayed part-ner's pain, leaving the man feeling isolated, judged, or misunderstood. While he must take responsibility for his actions, the therapy process also requires an acknowledgment of the broader dynamics in the rela-tionship and what might have led to the infidelity, though without excusing his choices.

The start of therapy is also a time when the man must navigate the painful task of recounting the details of the infidelity—either through confession or in response to his partner's questions. This process can feel like a minefield, as many men fear saying the wrong thing or revealing too much too soon, which can cause further hurt to their partner. They may struggle with how much to disclose, unsure of whether the truth will help or harm their chances of repairing the relationship. They are often avoidant for fear of sealing their fate. Unfortunately, this can create a drip of facts or "death by a thousand cuts." Every time another fact or reality is exposed, it brings the trauma back to the beginning. Men have to realize that parsing out the information over time does not help them. Therapy becomes a crucial guide in helping both partners navigate these early, treacherous conversations. It provides a structure for honesty while also working to contain the emotional fallout so that the couple can begin to find a way forward.

AFTER CRISIS, IN THERAPY: THE IMPORTANCE FOR BOTH PARTNERS OF DISTRESS TOLERANCE

Once the initial Crisis phase of infidelity recovery begins to subside, it becomes crucial to introduce the concept of "distress tolerance" for both partners. In the immediate aftermath of discovery or disclosure, emotions run high—shock, anger, grief, and guilt predominate. During this period, the betrayed partner is often focused on processing the pain, while the partner who committed the infidelity is consumed by guilt and the urgency to repair the damage. As the emotional intensity lessens and the relationship begins to stabilize, both partners need to shift their focus from crisis management to developing the emotional endurance necessary for the long-term work of recovery. This is where distress tolerance comes in as a key concept to help both individuals navigate the ongoing discomfort of the healing process.

Distress tolerance involves the ability to withstand difficult emotions without resorting to avoidance, denial, or destructive behavior. For the betrayed partner, it means learning to sit with their pain, anger, and distrust without constantly seeking immediate answers or reassurance. For the man who committed infidelity, it involves accepting the guilt and discomfort of facing his actions and the ongoing consequences without rushing to "fix" everything right away. Both partners will experience emotional triggers and moments of intense discomfort throughout the healing process, and building distress tolerance helps them stay engaged in the work without being overwhelmed by these moments. By introducing this concept in therapy, the therapist can help the couple develop a shared understanding that uncomfortable emotions are a part of the journey and that tolerating this discomfort is essential for long-term healing and growth.

The distinction between stress and distress is essential to understand, particularly in the context of infidelity recovery. Stress is primarily a physical response to external pressures or challenges, such as a tight deadline at work, financial strain, or an urgent need to solve a problem. It activates the body's fight-or-flight response, releasing hormones like adrenaline and cortisol, which prepare the body to act quickly. Stress, in this sense, can sometimes be positive, as it can motivate action and problem-solving in the short term.

Distress refers to the emotional and psychological pain that arises when an individual feels overwhelmed by difficult situations or emotions. Unlike physical stress, which can be mitigated by resolving the external problem, distress often involves deeper emotional turmoil, such as feelings of helplessness, shame, guilt, or sadness, that can linger even when external stressors are removed. In the context of infidelity recovery, distress is often a sustained emotional experience for both partners, involving a painful sense of betrayal, guilt, and grief that requires ongoing emotional processing. Building distress tolerance allows both individuals to engage with these uncomfortable emotions without being consumed by them, enabling healthier and more resilient coping over time.

Distress tolerance is not often a skill people have mastered, especially in moments of intense crisis. While many of us may be able to handle discomfort or frustration in our daily, mundane lives—whether it's dealing with a tough day at work, an argument with a friend, or an unexpected setback—those situations don't compare to the emotional upheaval that comes with a dire disruption like infidelity. In a crisis, emotions and fear can overwhelm even those who believe they have a strong capacity for coping. Usual methods for managing stress may no longer be effective, leaving both partners feeling pushed to their emotional and psychological limits. This is why developing and strengthening distress tolerance becomes critical in recovery work—it allows individuals to confront overwhelming emotions without shutting down, lashing out, or withdrawing entirely. In the aftermath of infidelity, where the stakes feel incredibly high, learning to stay present with these difficult emotions is essential for long-term healing.

Distress tolerance exists on a spectrum, and at its center lies a space of ease where individuals feel relatively comfortable but are not necessarily operating at their highest potential. In this middle zone, we can meet our basic goals and navigate daily tasks without significant difficulty, but we tend to do so without much effort or focus. This is a space where we may feel unfocused, inattentive, or even passive—going through the motions without being deeply engaged in the process. Indifference or apathy can settle in, and while we're not in a state of crisis, we're also not pushing ourselves to grow or fully face the challenges at hand. In this state of ease, we accomplish what is required, but often only at the most basic level, lacking the energy or intention to go beyond what's comfortable. While this middle ground can offer a sense of stability, it can also be a form of stagnation, preventing individuals from building resilience or expanding their capacity for handling more significant emotional or psychological demands. In the context of relationships, staying in this space may mean avoiding deeper conversations or growth opportunities that could lead to more meaningful connection and healing.

Moving outside the zone of ease (labeled "Content" in the graph) into a space of distress tolerance means stepping into a realm where we are actively challenged, but in a way that sharpens our focus and fuels our engagement. In this space, we are no longer coasting along

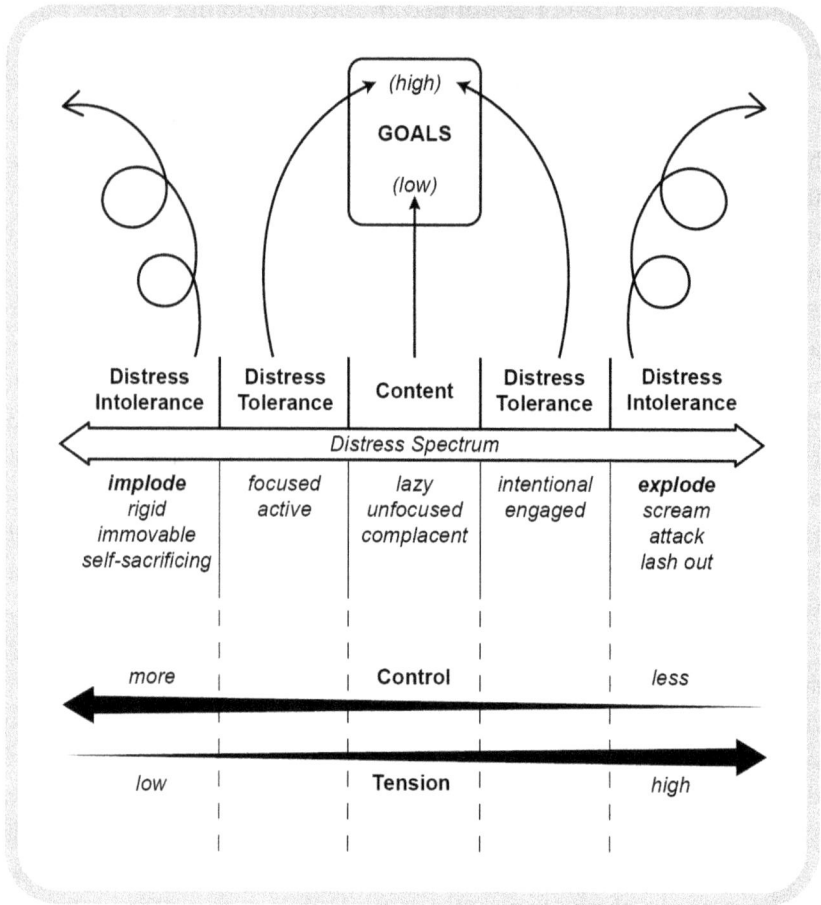

Distress Intolerance	Distress Tolerance	Content	Distress Tolerance	Distress Intolerance
		Distress Spectrum		
implode rigid immovable self-sacrificing	focused active	lazy unfocused complacent	intentional engaged	*explode* scream attack lash out
more		Control		less
low		Tension		high

Figure 4: **Distress Tolerance Spectrum**

passively but are instead operating with intention and curiosity. Our energy becomes directed toward growth, problem-solving, and deeper understanding. We're aware of the discomfort or emotional strain we might be experiencing, but rather than avoiding it, we lean into it with the purpose of learning and advancing. This heightened state of aware-ness helps us stay engaged and present, which allows us to achieve our goals with greater depth and quality.

When we operate in this zone of distress tolerance, whether we do so as part of infidelity recovery or as part of working with another source of distress, the effort we invest is more meaningful because it propels us beyond merely "getting by." In the zone of distress tolerance, we are impelled to reach for higher aspirations in our work, relationships, or personal growth, because the energy we're experiencing is put to good purpose. Whether we're using it to develop stronger communication in a partnership or tackle a professional challenge, our focus and engagement in this zone allow us to meet our goals more fully. It's a state where we're willing to stretch beyond what's comfortable, embracing the idea that growth happens when we challenge ourselves to think differently, to push through discomfort, and to pursue deeper insights and solutions.

When operating in the space of distress tolerance, it's natural to experience fatigue from the sustained effort and emotional engagement that comes with pushing ourselves beyond comfort. The focus, energy, and intention required can be mentally and emotionally draining, and there will be times when we need a break—a "vacation" from the hard work to recharge. Slipping back into the space of ease is not only normal but often necessary for self-care and rest. This allows us to step away from the intensity, reset our energy, and regain balance. However, the key is not to get stuck in that space of ease for too long, where passivity or avoidance can creep in. The goal is to take the rest we need, refresh ourselves, and then intentionally step back into being focused and engaged when we are ready. Balancing these periods of rest with periods of challenge helps sustain long-term growth and resilience, ensuring that we don't burn out but also don't become complacent in the process.

The space for distress tolerance during infidelity recovery is often constrained by the demands of daily life, leaving little room to process emotions or engage in the challenging work of healing. With responsibilities like caring for children, staying focused at work, and managing external commitments, a significant portion of one's emotional resilience is already used up. This leaves limited capacity to fully address the intense emotional strain of the affair, the relationship, or one's personal healing. Juggling these obligations means that distress tolerance is stretched thin, making it harder for both partners to stay present with their feelings or work through the recovery process without becoming overwhelmed.

In these circumstances, there's often little mental or emotional energy left for introspection or for engaging in the difficult conversations required in therapy. The pressure to maintain a façade of normalcy for children or colleagues can lead to exhaustion, pushing both partners back into survival mode rather than focusing on intentional recovery. This dynamic creates an even greater need for structure, self-care, and conscious time management, allowing space for each person to recharge and continue the difficult emotional work. Learning to prioritize recovery amidst the whirlwind of life's obligations is crucial to preventing burnout and ensuring that both partners have the resilience needed to navigate the journey of infidelity recovery.

The spectrum of distress tolerance is influenced by two opposing forces: control and tension. Control represents the desire to manage emotions, situations, or outcomes to maintain a sense of stability and predictability, while tension is the emotional and psychological strain that naturally arises when we encounter challenges, discomfort, or uncertainty. When control is high, individuals often feel a sense of calm, but too much control can lead to avoidance or rigidity, preventing growth. On the other hand, tension pushes us into unfamiliar or uncomfortable territory, which can foster growth but, when unchecked, may cause overwhelm or emotional fatigue.

At one end of the distress tolerance spectrum, when tension is high and control feels low, people often externalize their emotional responses. The overwhelming tension can lead to explosive reactions, where emotions bubble over and manifest as yelling, fighting, or lashing out at others. This externalization is an attempt to release the intense pressure and regain some semblance of control, though it often results in damaging interactions and conflict. These moments of emotional volatility arise because the person feels so powerless against the tension that the only option seems to be expressing it outwardly, in hopes of alleviating the internal discomfort.

On the opposite end of the spectrum, when someone tries to maintain tight control to avoid the discomfort of tension by avoiding the tension, they tend to internalize their reactions. In an effort to manage overwhelming emotions, they might freeze, become rigid, or even disassociate, disconnecting from the situation entirely. This internalization is a protective mechanism, but it can create a sense of emotional distance or numbness. While this may provide temporary relief from the tension, it also prevents genuine engagement with the underlying issues, leading to feelings of isolation and stunted emotional growth. In both extremes, the individual's ability to tolerate distress is compromised, and the challenge lies in finding a balance where they can engage with the tension without losing control or shutting down.

The ultimate goal in the recovery process is to expand the space of distress tolerance for both partners, fostering resilience that enables them to navigate the emotional complexities of infidelity while maintaining a supportive relationship. By strategically utilizing the space of ease, both partners can take necessary breaks from intense emotional work, allowing themselves moments of respite and recovery without completely retreating into avoidance or complacency. This balanced approach encourages them to engage in self-care and recharge, so they can approach the distress tolerance space with renewed energy and focus. As they gradually build their resilience, they become more capable of facing challenges together, transforming their relationship dynamics into a healthier, more connected partnership that thrives on mutual understanding and support, rather than fear and tension.

৵৵৲

Infidelity recovery is a profoundly challenging process, but it offers an opportunity for growth and transformation when both partners commit to the work. For the man who committed infidelity, this journey begins with accountability—understanding the impact of his actions, addressing his internal conflicts, and recognizing the broader relational patterns that contributed to the betrayal. This process requires emotional courage and the willingness to dismantle the compartmentalization that once enabled the affair, replacing it with authenticity and transparency in the primary relationship.

For the betrayed partner, healing involves navigating the shock and pain of betrayal while gradually exploring the relationship's complexities. Acknowledging the role of relational dynamics is not about shifting blame but rather about creating a fuller picture of what went wrong and how both partners can move forward. This dual focus on personal responsibility and shared relational work allows both individuals to confront the rupture and begin rebuilding trust and intimacy.

For the clinician facilitating the process, the ability to identify the relational dynamics, the presence of disenfranchised grief, and grow distress tolerance with both partners, while collaborating with the additional resources the couple is using for healing, is a tremendous amount of work. It requires a deep well of skill, awareness, and compassion for the emotional intensity of the journey.

Ultimately, infidelity recovery requires expanding each partner's ability to tolerate emotional distress while remaining connected to one another. By fostering resilience and creating space for vulnerability, the couple can transform the aftermath of betrayal into an opportunity for deeper understanding and connection. Though the path is arduous, it is one that holds the potential for lasting growth and a redefined partnership built on mutual intention and curiosity.

PART II

▼

INTERVENTION

∽

Healing doesn't mean the damage never existed. It means the damage no longer controls our lives.

—Akshay Dubey

8

▼

A HOPEFUL FUTURE

Infidelity, with all its pain and complexity, doesn't have to signal the end of your relationship. While the betrayal can feel overwhelming, if both partners are genuinely willing and capable of doing the difficult healing work, it can lead to a deeper, more meaningful connection. Through honest communication, rebuilding trust, and confronting vulnerabilities, couples can emerge stronger, with a foundation rooted in security and authenticity. The process is neither quick nor easy, but with commitment and time, the relationship can transform from one of hurt and mistrust into one of profound honesty and mutual respect. Healing is possible, and it can lead to a renewed bond that thrives on genuine understanding and shared growth.

Both partners must hold onto hope and be willing to explore their own vulnerabilities, hurts, and deeper desires if they are to heal from infidelity. This means looking inward to acknowledge personal shortcomings, emotional wounds, and the ways each contributed to the relationship's previous challenges. It's not just about addressing the betrayal itself but also understanding the broader dynamics that may have led to disconnection. A genuine desire to rebuild the relationship is essential; both partners must be committed to staying present in the process, facing uncomfortable truths, and opening up to one another with honesty. This mutual willingness creates the possibility of forging a stronger, more resilient bond, one that is fortified by the clarity and depth that comes from confronting these difficult emotions together.

Ending the relationship is a very real and valid option, and for some couples, it may ultimately be the healthiest choice. However, it's crucial that this decision isn't made in the heat of the moment or as a knee-jerk reaction to the pain of discovery. Deciding to separate should come after thoughtful reflection, honest dialogue, and, ideally, a clear understanding of what both partners need and want moving forward. Rushing to end things prematurely can leave unresolved emotions and missed opportunities for growth, whether that growth happens together or apart. Taking the time to explore all options—both staying and leaving—allows for a more informed and intentional decision that aligns with each partner's well-being and long-term goals.

CASE STUDY

ALAN AND CAROL

Alan and Carol had been married for 22 years, raising two adolescent children together. From the outside, their life appeared stable, but beneath the surface, Alan had been struggling with a long-standing issue—he had been visiting massage parlors for years. The secrecy of his behavior weighed on him, but he had compartmentalized it, convincing himself that he could manage his kink and it wouldn't affect his family. However, everything came crashing down one afternoon when Carol discovered a receipt in Alan's car. It was from a massage service, and her suspicions immediately rose and she started investigating—with devastating results.

When Carol confronted Alan, he initially denied everything, trying to downplay the situation. But Carol wasn't convinced and pushed harder, challenging his denial with her

Continued

unwavering resolve. Faced with her determination and his mounting guilt, Alan finally broke down. Through tears, he confessed to his years of secret behavior, revealing the full extent of his actions. The weight of his confession left Carol devastated, and Alan could no longer hide from the pain and betrayal he had caused. It was the beginning of a long, painful process of reckoning for both of them, with deep wounds now fully exposed.

Alan's confession marked a turning point in his life, one that led him to seek help in ways he had never before considered. He joined a 12-step program, Sex and Love Addicts Anonymous (SLAA), where he began confronting the roots of his compulsive behaviors. In addition, Alan started individual therapy, which revealed layers of unresolved trauma from his own childhood sexual abuse, an experience that began in the context of massage. For the first time, Alan was able to connect his past trauma with his present behavior, recognizing how it had fueled his unhealthy coping mechanisms. This work was scary for Alan as he had to admit that his core relationships with certain family members needed to be reconsidered. As he uncovered how these events stunted many aspects of his life, he became depressed, layering on the issues he had to face at the same time.

It was both the childhood trauma and the infidelity that were deep roots for Alan's disenfranchised grief. Growing up, Alan was told, and he believed, that being sexual at such an early age made him a man and, in some ways, more advanced than his friends. He viewed his sexual behaviors with a sense of pride—that he was knowledgeable and adept in the ways of sexual pleasure. He then began to believe that one of his greatest values to others was his sexual skill. The discovery of his infidelity brought a new awareness to Alan. Alan struggled with the reality that his childhood was not one of safety and nurturance but rather abuse and pain. He had to wrestle with the dichotomy that the physical feelings he received during his

Continued

abuse might have felt good and, at the same time, set a course of sexual acting out in the future. He had to face the reality that he was not able to link sex with emotional connection, and the sex workers he was seeing at the massage parlor were paid to tell him what a wonderful lover he was. When Carol discovered the full extent of his secrets, the truth of their sexual and emotional disconnection was put on full display. This journey of self-awareness and accountability was difficult, but it was necessary for him to begin healing. As Alan struggled to come to terms that his past was not how he valued it, it became even more difficult to talk to Carol about the emotional challenges he was facing in his treatment.

As Alan progressed in his individual treatment, working through his shame and the deep-seated pain from his childhood, Carol slowly began to see changes in him. Although still hurt and wary, she recognized his genuine efforts to understand the root of his behavior and take responsibility for his actions. It was only then that they decided to start couples therapy, embarking on the challenging path of recovery from his infidelity. The couples work was emotional and raw, but it provided a space where they could begin to rebuild trust, communicate honestly, and explore the underlying dynamics of their relationship. Both were able to better understand the challenges Alan was having reconciling his past while acknowledging the pain he caused. Through their joint efforts, they sought to heal not only from the betrayal but also from the years of unspoken pain that had affected both of them.

The work of couples therapy was deeply challenging for Carol, as her anger and hurt ran intensely deep. Each session brought new waves of emotion—while she felt justified in her outrage and betrayal, she also wrestled with an unexpected empathy for Alan. As she learned more about the trauma he had endured as a child, Carol found herself torn between her own pain and a growing sense of care and concern for what Alan had lived through. It was confusing and overwhelming to

Continued

hold space for both her suffering and Alan's, and she struggled to reconcile her feelings of compassion with the deep wounds his actions had inflicted on her. This inner conflict became a key part of her journey in therapy, as she worked through how to honor her hurt while still moving toward healing together.

Coordinating care between Alan's and Carol's individual therapists was crucial to the progress they made in couples therapy. Each of them was facing their own personal battles— Alan was confronting the trauma of his past and the shame of his actions, while Carol was processing the deep betrayal and emotional fallout from the infidelity. Without alignment between their individual therapists and the couples work, the healing process could have felt fragmented, with each person focused only on their own pain. However, when all the therapists began to coordinate and align the goals of treatment, a more unified approach emerged.

This coordination allowed Alan and Carol to work on their individual hurts while simultaneously developing healthier communication and stronger boundaries in their relationship. Alan was able to find language to express his remorse without feeling overwhelmed by his shame, while Carol could voice her anger without being swallowed by it. Over time, they learned to hold space for one another's emotions—a key shift that created room for deeper understanding. It was with the help of this careful integration of individual and couples therapy that they could begin rebuilding trust, learning to navigate their shared future with a new foundation of respect and emotional support.

This work was slow and arduous. Alan and Carol spent five years in couples therapy before they reached a point where they felt stable enough to bring that chapter of their therapeutic journey to a close. The work continued and was not linear—there were setbacks, moments of doubt, and times when both of them felt like giving up. But through persistent effort, they gradually rebuilt their relationship on a foundation of honesty, trust, and mutual understanding. Even after

Continued

completing couples therapy, they remained committed to their individual work, with Carol continuing to process her pain and Alan diving deeper into healing from his childhood abuse.

As Alan's work in individual therapy progressed, he began to feel that the core issues driving his behaviors were being addressed. His attendance at 12-step meetings began to wane as he found more resolution in understanding and healing his childhood trauma. For Carol, the journey was also ongoing, as she worked to restore her sense of self and her ability to trust again. Despite the progress they had made, they remained vigilant, returning to couples therapy periodically for "check-ups" to ensure their bond stayed healthy and strong. These shorter, focused sessions were crucial in reinforcing the skills they had developed and in ensuring that they continued to nurture their relationship rather than fall into old patterns.

CASE STUDY

Brett and Michelle

Brett and Michelle had been married for 18 years, raising two teenage children together. They had built a seemingly stable life, with the usual challenges of work, parenting, and managing their busy household. One evening, Michelle picked up Brett's iPad to check something, only to find a messaging app left open. Her curiosity turned to horror as she scrolled through the messages and pictures that revealed Brett had been paying a dominatrix regularly. The content was shocking—detailed descriptions of BDSM (Bondage/Discipline/Dominance/Sub-

Continued

mission/Sadomasochism), photos, and conversations that unveiled a hidden side of Brett that Michelle never knew existed. The strong, bold, vibrant husband she thought she was married to was engaging in submissive sex with a sex worker. She didn't even recognize her husband in the photos.

When Michelle confronted Brett in a fit of rage, her emotions were overwhelming—shock, anger, and deep betrayal flooded every interaction. She demanded answers, her voice trembling with hurt as she asked him how long this had been going on, why he had done this when their sex life was practically nonexistent, and if their entire marriage had been a lie. But Brett, overwhelmed and paralyzed by the weight of what had been exposed, became numb. His only response to each of Michelle's questions was, "I don't know ... I don't know." It was as if he was unable to access any explanation or emotion, retreating further into himself, which only fueled Michelle's fury and confusion. The disconnect between her pain and his inability to respond only deepened the hurt in their already devastated relationship.

Brett and Michelle came to couples therapy in a state of deep crisis, their relationship teetering on the edge after Michelle's devastating discovery. Michelle made Brett move out of the house and he was living in a hotel. Their teenage children were told that Brett had cheated and was not in the house. Their kids became enraged at Brett, siding with Michelle as she would be inconsolable and often crying in her bedroom.

In that first session, it was clear that they needed immediate support not just as a couple but as individuals, with their own distinct emotional needs. The intensity of Michelle's rage and Brett's numbness made it clear that each of them had personal work to do alongside their couples therapy. To ensure they could process their feelings in a safe space, they both agreed to seek individual therapy, where they could explore their personal struggles without fear of immediate repercussions within the relationship.

Continued

As part of the therapeutic plan, it was essential that the clinicians collaborate while respecting the confidentiality of Brett and Michelle's individual sessions. This collaboration ensured that both individual and couples therapy would be aligned in terms of overarching goals, but it also allowed Brett and Michelle the freedom to explore their raw emotions privately. If either was not yet ready to share specific details or feelings with their partner, they could do so in the sanctuary of their own therapy, knowing that their individual healing was an essential step toward any hope of relational repair. This balance of collaboration and confidentiality created a space where both partners could feel supported and respected while navigating the immense challenges of infidelity recovery.

Early in the couples work, it became evident that both Brett and Michelle were grappling with rigid black-and-white thinking, which severely limited their ability to envision a future together. Michelle's experiences of betrayal with a previous partner had left her feeling vulnerable and distrustful, causing her to see Brett's infidelity as a definitive sign of his unworthiness. Meanwhile, Brett's long-time inability to express his sexual fantasies had led him to compartmentalize his desires, leading to a sense of shame and secrecy that shut him down from connection with Michelle and fueled the crisis. This stark separation of thought—the idea that either they could fully restore their relationship or that it was irrevocably broken—created a barrier to meaningful dialogue and healing.

To address these deeply entrenched narratives, the collaboration between their individual therapists became critically important. While Michelle worked through her feelings of betrayal and past hurts, Brett was encouraged to explore the roots of his sexual desires and the fears that had kept him from expressing them. In couples therapy, the focus shifted to creating a safe environment where both partners could begin to articulate their thoughts and feelings without fear of judgment or rejection. Both partners, in spite of the intensity, were

Continued

open to seeing what the marriage could be remade into. The first step was to communicate to their children that they were working on the marriage and both wanted their support. Brett moved back into the house after a month and stayed in the guest room. Helping Brett and Michelle navigate this transition was tricky as both wanted to support their children, while holding boundaries so the children did not insert themselves into the private work Brett and Michelle had to face.

Couples therapy allowed them to slowly develop new relational skills based on the realities they discovered through their individual work. Over time, they learned to challenge their rigid beliefs, recognizing that relationships can exist in a wider spectrum of possibility, allowing for growth, understanding, and ultimately, a more profound connection. After four months, Brett moved back into the bedroom, but touch was still verboten.

Brett found himself in a deeply vulnerable position, feeling the weight of being labeled a "kinky perv" after Michelle discovered his secret life. Disenfranchised grief was explored when Brett felt that his submissive sexual cravings diminished who he was in Michelle's eyes and to a greater extent, the world. When his sexual desires were found out, Brett believed that no one could understand him, that no one would respect him as a man any longer, and Michelle—who offered to explore this play with him—was only pacifying him. This sense of deep exposure compounded his feelings of shame and inadequacy, feeling he was in a "one-down" position where he felt he had no recourse but to acquiesce to Michelle's every demand and concern. He believed that by saying "yes" to everything she requested—whether it was assurances of fidelity, transparency about his feelings that he was having challenges accessing, or commitments to how the marriage would look in the future— he could somehow regain her trust and alleviate her pain. However, this approach quickly proved to be problematic.

As Brett attempted to meet Michelle's needs with a series

Continued

of affirmations, he soon discovered that he couldn't deliver on all these "yeses." This inability to fulfill her expectations only intensified Michelle's hurt and outrage, leading to a cycle of blame and frustration. She began to perceive Brett's compliance not as a sign of his commitment to the relationship, but rather as an indication of his lack of commitment to growth and his ineffectiveness in truly understanding her pain or addressing the complexities of their situation. In therapy, it became essential to help Brett navigate his feelings of inadequacy and empower him to express his own needs and limitations while at the same time helping Michelle to invite curiosity in the space of her pain. The couple had to learn that true intimacy requires more than just compliance; it demands open communication, vulnerability, and the acknowledgment of each partner's realities, paving the way for authentic healing and connection.

As Brett and Michelle gradually emerged from the crisis phase of their relationship, it became increasingly clear that their marriage had been unbalanced for years. Brett had focused primarily on his work, which led him to abdicate responsibility for the relationship's emotional and relational health, leaving Michelle to carry much of the burden. This imbalance not only caused resentment but also stunted their ability to engage in meaningful conversations about their needs and desires. Consequently, when Brett finally faced relationship concerns, he was at a loss as to how to effectively communicate those feelings to Michelle or to involve her in the challenging work of building a true partnership.

In couples therapy, they began to reshape their relationship by creating a "new marriage" that incorporated new dynamics, skills, and expectations. It took over two years of intense couple work for Brett to reconcile his sexual desires and realize that he could also have different forms of sex with Michelle that were meaningful. Her willingness to explore his fetishes seemed to reduce his desire to play in that way. As they

Continued

progressed, Brett began to better understand that much of his submissive sexual desire was linked to the disconnects and pressures he felt in his life. While submissive play was normalized and accepted into the marriage, Brett felt less inclined to want it.

This process was not without its challenges; both partners were required to engage in deep self-reflection and confront uncomfortable truths about their past behaviors and patterns. They delved into their old scripts—patterns of interaction that had become automatic over the years—and examined the triggers and expectations that had been established not only within their marriage but also stemming from their earlier life experiences. This transformative work was taxing for both Brett and Michelle, as it forced them to confront painful memories and long-held beliefs about themselves and each other. Yet, through this laborious process, they discovered a path toward greater intimacy and understanding, ultimately leading them to develop a toolbox for solving problems, having hard conversations, and creating a shared vision of what the future could be.

CASE STUDY

SHAWN

Shawn found himself in a complex emotional landscape after engaging in a long-term affair with a coworker. Initially, this extramarital relationship served as a welcome escape from the disconnection he felt in his marriage. With no children to bind

Continued

them, Shawn and his wife had drifted into a comfortable yet stagnant routine, one that lacked the intimacy and passion he yearned for. Despite loving his wife, he sensed that she had become more of a close friend than a romantic partner. The affair, at first, felt exhilarating, offering him the distraction and validation he craved. It filled a void, providing excitement and attention that he believed was missing in his marriage.

However, as the years rolled on, Shawn began to feel the weight of the affair's complexities. What initially seemed like a straightforward escape turned into a source of anxiety and conflict. He found himself just saying the words and phrases that his affair partner wanted to hear even though they were not true. He described it as "just reading from a play script ... just say the lines ... don't think about it ... and then move on." This absentminded approach seemed to keep his affair partner happy and content and allowed him to avoid the reality of his own unhappiness in this relationship. His affair partner, who once embodied the thrill he sought, started expressing desires for a deeper commitment—something Shawn was not prepared to offer. This newfound pressure weighed heavily on him, leading to feelings of guilt and internal conflict. He longed to reconnect with his wife but found himself trapped in a web of deception and emotional turmoil. The affair was now the painful relationship that he wanted to escape from as he started to see his wife as the desired connection. As he contemplated ending the affair, Shawn wrestled with the daunting reality of addressing the rift in his marriage. The relief he once found in the affair now felt overshadowed by the burden of his choices, prompting him to seek a way out of the duplicity and towards a more authentic path.

When Shawn mustered the courage to confront his affair partner and express his desire to end their relationship, he was taken aback by her vehement refusal. "No," she said firmly, her voice tinged with an angry ultimatum. If he attempted to sever ties, she threatened to disclose the affair to his wife,

Continued

weaponizing the intimate details against him. This revelation sent shockwaves through Shawn, stirring an intense fear that compounded his already tumultuous emotions. He was acutely aware of his wife's struggles with depression and the devastating impact such betrayal could have on her mental health. The thought of losing not just his marriage but also his best friend pushed him into a state of panic, leaving him feeling trapped in a situation he had never anticipated.

As the tension escalated, Shawn found himself wrestling with feelings of resentment toward his affair partner, whose demands and threats felt increasingly suffocating. He was caught in a relentless cycle of guilt, fear, and obligation, forced to navigate a treacherous landscape of deception and emotional turmoil. To complicate matters further, the fact that she was a coworker added another layer of stress—he feared that she could easily undermine his professional life as well. This looming threat of exposure, both personal and professional, propelled Shawn to seek help through individual therapy. In this safe space, he began to unpack the emotional weight of his choices, confront the dynamics of his affair, and explore a path toward reclaiming his integrity and finding a way to reconnect with his wife.

In a particularly intense therapy session, Shawn revealed a startling revelation: he had spotted his affair partner in a local coffee shop, conversing with his wife. The sight of them together sent him into a whirlwind of emotions, igniting a spark of determination he hadn't felt in a long time. As he recounted the moment, the weight of his secrets began to feel unbearably heavy. In that emotionally charged space, Shawn declared his intention to come clean to his wife. "It's best that she hears it from me," he stated, his voice trembling with both fear and resolve. He realized that by withholding the truth, he had inadvertently given power to his affair partner. This was his opportunity to reclaim his agency and ownership of his choices, regardless of the potential fallout.

Continued

That weekend, with the memory of his therapy session still echoing in his mind, Shawn took the monumental step of disclosing his long-standing affair to his wife. As he sat across from her, words spilling out amidst tears and tremors, he could see the shock and devastation wash over her face. Each revelation cut through the silence of their once-harmonious relationship, and the gravity of his confession hung heavy in the air. However, within that moment of honesty, Shawn felt a strange sense of liberation. Though he understood the pain he was causing, he recognized that confronting the truth was the first step toward healing, not just for himself but for his wife as well. He had taken back control of his narrative, paving the way for an uncertain but necessary journey toward rebuilding trust and intimacy in their marriage.

In the aftermath of Shawn's confession, his wife confronted the reality of their situation with a mix of hurt and resilience. While she felt deeply wounded by his actions, she made it clear that she wanted to remain in the marriage. However, she drew a firm line, stating that she refused to engage in any couples or individual therapy. "This is not my problem," she insisted, emphasizing her desire to navigate the emotional fallout on her own terms. Although she no longer desired to share sexual intimacy with Shawn, she recognized the value of their friendship and the life they had built together over the years. Their shared history was precious to her, a foundation she wasn't ready to abandon despite the betrayal.

Faced with this new reality, Shawn found himself at a crossroads. He could choose to remain in a marriage that lacked sexual and erotic intimacy, but was filled with deep affection and companionship, or he could opt to leave and pursue a different path. Shawn inquired about options for a non-monogamous marriage. His wife told him that she could not tolerate that. He could choose to stay but his infidelity would never be tolerated again. After much contemplation, Shawn made the decision to stay. In his eyes, the emotional

Continued

connection they shared held significant value, even in the absence of physical intimacy. He began to describe their marriage as sexually lonely, acknowledging the gap where desire used to thrive. However, he found ways to take care of his own needs without crossing the boundaries they had established. Ultimately, Shawn discovered that the love and appreciation they expressed for one another brought him a sense of fulfillment that he hadn't anticipated, redefining what it meant to be in a meaningful partnership. For Shawn, the grief over the loss of his erotic partnership remains but he is no longer disenfranchised as he has been able to talk about the pain it causes and the reality that he made a choice to choose that path.

CASE STUDY

DEREK AND JENNA

Derek is a friendly, easy-going guy with a natural knack for making people feel comfortable, and he's always been that way. Married to his college sweetheart, Jenna, he'd carved out a life that, on the outside, looked stable and wholesome. They have three adolescent kids, all heavily involved in sports, music, and school activities, keeping the family calendar packed year-round. Derek was the dad who knew all his kids' friends, stayed for every game, and always made time to help Jenna with her packed schedule. Yet, behind the scenes, he carried an internal struggle that even he didn't fully understand at first.

The affair began slowly, almost innocently, or so he told himself at first. He wasn't looking for a fling or another rela-

Continued

tionship, but he found himself drawn to the ease of his connection with someone who wasn't asking him for anything but his company. The texts with his affair partner started as light-hearted, flirtatious exchanges, becoming a habit he could slip into without facing the weight of his life at home. It felt freeing, unburdened by history or unmet expectations, a place where he could just be Derek. And at that time, he told himself it was just "something for himself"—a small rebellion in a life that had come to feel overly dictated by everyone else's needs.

When Jenna first found the messages, Derek was shaken but defensive. He minimized the affair, told her it was no big deal, and assured her it was over, wanting to calm the storm as quickly as it had come. But he couldn't seem to leave the affair behind. Jenna discovered his continued contact with the affair partner two more times after that, each time more explosive than the last. At this point, she laid it out clearly: if he didn't stop, they were done. The threat of truly losing his family—something he genuinely loved and valued—jolted him. For the first time, he let himself question why he'd risked it all in the first place.

Through difficult, honest conversations in therapy, Derek was finally able to put words to feelings he'd kept hidden. He discussed feeling like he was always at the bottom of the list, his needs brushed aside while he kept up with the seemingly endless obligations of their family life. Jenna, he admitted, often felt emotionally unavailable, locked into her own routines and schedules. He resented feeling trapped, like he was a spectator in his own life, tasked with everyone else's happiness but left with no time or space to pursue his own.

Reflecting on it now, Derek sees how he'd mistaken the affair for a solution, a quick fix that allowed him to feel seen without actually doing the hard work of communicating with Jenna. He understands that his resentment was building a wall between them. It wasn't fair to expect Jenna to read his mind, just as it wasn't fair to keep that part of his life hidden from her. Ending the affair felt like removing a crutch, forcing him

Continued

to lean into his marriage again, this time with a commitment to being honest about his needs. Now, Derek is focused on making changes that don't rely on temporary escapes, hoping he and Jenna can rebuild something deeper, built on more than a shared history and mutual obligations.

In the aftermath of everything coming to light, Derek wrestled with the heavy, lingering thought that Jenna would never fully forgive him. He'd always been the man people leaned on—reliable, steady, the guy friends could call at two in the morning and know he'd show up. He took pride in being Jenna's rock, the one she could count on through thick and thin. But now, with the affair exposed, he felt like he'd shattered that image, broken the very core of who he thought he was. The guilt was relentless, and every time Jenna looked at him with that mix of pain and anger, it dug the knife deeper, reinforcing the belief that he'd lost her trust for good.

When Jenna agreed to join him in couples therapy, Derek felt a cautious relief. Part of him hoped it would be a fast path to forgiveness—that maybe, through therapy, she'd find a way to move past her hurt, and they could restore what they'd once had. But every session brought more uncomfortable truths to the surface. Jenna's pain wasn't something that would disappear with apologies, no matter how sincere, or reassurances, no matter how convincing. She showed up each time with her wounds still raw, and her reactivity would flare up at even the slightest hint of him brushing things off. She wasn't just hurt; she felt profoundly insecure in the relationship, like the foundation had been yanked out from under her.

Derek struggled to separate the idea of forgiveness from security. In his mind, if Jenna was still angry, still hurt, it meant she hadn't forgiven him. He didn't realize how desperately he'd been searching for signs that he could move past his shame, that he could be forgiven, and maybe even rebuild his sense of self. But he missed the key piece: forgiveness wasn't about erasing her feelings. Forgiveness, he began to under-

Continued

stand, could coexist with insecurity, and her commitment to staying in the marriage, despite everything, was evidence that she was working toward forgiving him in her own way.

It was a pivotal moment when he could see the difference. Jenna's staying wasn't a sign that everything was back to normal or that she felt safe with him yet. Her staying meant she was open to rebuilding trust, but the work of creating security had to come from him. This was a revelation. Derek realized he'd been asking Jenna to reassure him that he was forgiven, yet he'd neglected the effort needed to rebuild her sense of safety. Her reactivity wasn't a refusal to forgive—it was an outcry over feeling vulnerable and unprotected in their relationship.

From then on, Derek stopped focusing on whether or not she forgave him and, instead, began prioritizing ways to make her feel secure again. He started to truly listen, resisting the urge to defend himself, and approached her pain as an opportunity to learn what she needed from him, not as something he needed to "fix." With each small effort to show up for her, even in the face of her anger or hurt, Derek felt the possibility of restoring a deeper connection, one that honored the struggle they'd been through and the commitment they both still held.

CASE STUDY

MATTHEW

Matthew's earliest memories of family life were ones of uncertainty and confusion. His parents divorced while he was still in elementary school, and even then, he understood more than most kids his age. He knew his father had cheated on

Continued

his mother—not just once, but many times. And it wasn't just the betrayals; his father's infidelities had resulted in a second family, a discovery that shook Matthew's young world. After the divorce, his father wasn't around much, and his mother, though doing her best, was often exhausted and emotionally drained. As a result, Matthew learned to fend for himself, becoming self-sufficient far too young.

When Matthew got a summer job at a warehouse in his early teens, it offered him a paycheck and an escape from the solitude at home. But it also exposed him to a very different side of adulthood. The men he worked with were rough and spoke openly about sex in ways that were blunt and demeaning. The office walls were plastered with pornographic posters, images that made him curious. They'd often watch porn on the office computer, laughing and nudging each other as if it were just part of the workday. To them, women weren't people but objects, the punchlines of their jokes, the goals of their bragging rights.

As the youngest there, Matthew quickly realized he was expected to fit in and follow their example if he wanted their approval. They encouraged him to "man up," nudging him toward viewing relationships in the same detached, transactional way they did. He soon found himself emulating them, seeking out casual encounters without attachment, chasing the thrill of experiences he didn't yet fully understand. This mindset became ingrained, an unchallenged part of how he moved through relationships, leaving him adrift when it came to developing meaningful connections.

This early exposure to a distorted view of manhood and intimacy would follow Matthew into adulthood, shaping how he understood relationships and fulfillment. While he found love and stability later in life, his early experiences left him grappling with conflicting ideas about commitment, leaving him vulnerable to old patterns that would surface in unexpected ways.

Continued

When Matthew met Diana, he was captivated. She was grounded and had a warmth that steadied him in ways he hadn't known he needed. For the first time, he felt like he had someone he could rely on, a partner with whom he could build something meaningful. They eventually married and settled into a life that was stable, loving, and monogamous—a welcome contrast to the chaotic relationships he'd known before. For several years, things were good between them, and they shared a fulfilling sex life that, for a time, kept him satisfied.

Yet as their life together grew more routine, Matthew began to feel the pull of old patterns. Due to executive functioning challenges, he often struggled with the structure of their daily lives, finding it difficult to keep up with schedules and responsibilities without feeling drained. As time went on, even their intimacy, while plentiful, started to feel predictable. He missed the "wild and exciting" feelings he'd chased in his past, memories that started creeping back in when the monotony of day-to-day life settled in.

One night, while browsing online, he stumbled into a chat room, which led to casual conversations that quickly turned flirtatious. The excitement grew with each message, a rush that felt freeing and exhilarating in ways he hadn't felt in a long time. Soon, the chats turned into something more, and he began meeting up with people he'd met online, keeping these hookups separate from his marriage in his mind, compartmentalizing them as something that had "nothing to do" with his relationship with Diana.

Eventually, though, Diana discovered his social media and read through the messages he'd exchanged with other people. Seeing the explicitness and the extent of his interactions, she was horrified. She confronted him, and when he tried to explain it away, her devastation only deepened. Feeling betrayed beyond repair, she demanded a divorce.

But financial circumstances kept them in the same house, forcing them into a painfully awkward coexistence. Desperate

Continued

to salvage any chance he had, Matthew begged Diana to let him try to make amends. He promised to join Sex and Love Addicts Anonymous and start therapy, committing to both if she would consider staying. With guarded agreement, Diana moved into the guest room, and Matthew began his journey to understand his past and break from the patterns he'd carried with him for so long.

Matthew's journey in therapy was raw and intense, as he faced parts of himself he'd long buried beneath a façade of bravado and detachment. At first, he came to therapy out of desperation—to save his marriage and to prove that he was different from his father. But as he leaned into the work, he realized that this was a deeper opportunity to redefine himself, to become the kind of partner he wanted to be, and ultimately, to let go of the shame and confusion he had carried since he was a teenager.

Unpacking his past was painful. With guidance, Matthew began to recognize the messages from his childhood that had shaped his understanding of love and intimacy. He'd grown up without a model for healthy attachment, absorbing instead the belief that love was unreliable, that sex was a way to prove his worth, and that real connection was something out of reach. For years, he'd believed the men in the warehouse when they told him that his exploits would make him a "real man," yet now, with the clarity of self-reflection, he began to feel the weight of a disenfranchised grief. This wasn't just guilt over what he'd done to Diana—it was a profound sadness for the boy he'd been, who had conflated affection with conquest, who was praised for physical pursuits but starved of emotional connection.

Therapy helped him understand that much of his behavior had been driven by a fractured need to feel valued and loved, needs he had previously channeled through empty encounters that ultimately left him feeling hollow. Learning how to connect love with sex was a new challenge for him, and one

Continued

he took seriously, recognizing that he would need to let go of his old "stud" persona to grow into someone who genuinely admired and valued the intimacy he could share with Diana.

Therapy also helped him see that healing wasn't just about winning back Diana's trust but also about supporting her through her own pain. As he began to share his story with her—giving her the context of his past, his misguided beliefs, and his fears—Diana was able to see him more clearly, understanding the roots of his struggles even if they still hurt her. This openness brought a new depth to their conversations, helping them both work toward healing. He committed to rebuilding their relationship from the ground up, focusing on new relationship skills that emphasized transparency, compassion, and honesty.

Over time, Matthew grieved the person he once thought he had to be, letting go of the mask he'd worn for so long. In doing so, he created space for a new self to emerge, a man who valued true connection over surface-level validation, who honored love as something deeper than excitement. Slowly, Matthew became someone he could admire, and through this journey, he began to cultivate a sense of worth and identity that was finally his own.

CASE STUDY

DAVID AND SARAH

David grew up in a house filled with tension and uncertainty, shaped by his father's alcoholism and his mother's persistent anxiety and depression. As the youngest of three children, he often felt overlooked, left to figure out life on his own while

Continued

chaos unfolded around him. His siblings were older and preoc-
cupied with escaping the household as soon as they could, and
David spent much of his childhood just trying to stay under
the radar. He learned early on to keep his feelings to himself,
developing a coping mechanism of "just moving forward"
without addressing the emotions beneath.

When he met Sarah, he thought he'd found his escape,
a safe haven where he could finally build a calm, predictable
life. Their relationship was warm and easy, a soothing balm
for his chaotic past. Marriage felt like the ultimate reassurance
that he could live a different kind of life, one without drama,
where they could rely on each other unconditionally. For the
first time, David felt like he had found true stability—a refuge
he'd longed for as a child.

In the early years, things were as he'd hoped. They shared
laughter, routines, and dreams about their future family. But as
time passed and they tried to have children, they encountered
heartbreak after heartbreak, enduring several miscarriages.
Each one hit Sarah deeply, leaving her grieving and withdrawn,
searching for answers and comfort. David, however, felt paralyzed by her pain. He had no experience in dealing with emotions so raw, and, not knowing how to comfort her, he chose to
retreat into himself instead. He stuck to his coping strategy—
keeping his head down, pressing forward, convincing himself
that if they just moved on, things would eventually get better.

David and Sarah carried the silent burden of disenfranchised grief from their infertility struggles, a sorrow that felt
invisible to the world around them. While others seemed to
move forward with families of their own, David and Sarah
faced repeated losses that remained largely unacknowledged by
society. Friends and family, unsure of how to respond or unaware
of the depth of their pain, often offered platitudes or avoided
the topic altogether, leaving David and Sarah feeling isolated in
their grief. For David, who had never learned how to process or
express his emotions, this grief only deepened his retreat, com-

Continued

pounding the shame he felt for not being able to "fix" things for Sarah. Meanwhile, Sarah mourned not only their losses but the shared dreams of parenthood they were gradually forced to relinquish. With few outlets for their sorrow, their pain became unspoken, a quiet presence between them that only widened the emotional distance in their marriage.

And the space between them grew. Sarah's grief was isolating, and David's silence felt like abandonment to her. She wanted him to acknowledge the loss and share in her sorrow, but David didn't know how to enter that space with her. For him, emotions were complicated, best kept at a distance, and his instinct was to avoid rather than confront. His unspoken hope was that if he didn't focus on the pain, it would disappear on its own.

Yet, beneath the surface, David felt the weight of their losses, and his inability to support Sarah in the way she needed filled him with a gnawing sense of guilt and inadequacy. He wondered if he was truly the husband he'd promised to be, if he could ever be the partner she needed. But for now, he clung to his old habits, hoping that somehow things would resolve on their own, unaware of the growing distance that lay between them. This loss of his desired identity only served to deepen his disenfranchised grief.

Feeling increasingly alone in his grief, David found himself drawn to Blaire, the wife of one of his friends. Blaire's easygoing presence offered an escape from the unspoken tension at home, a place where David could relax without the weight of unexpressed sorrow hanging over him. Their conversations started off casual, just friendly check-ins and laughter about lighthearted things. But as time went on, David began texting Blaire with greater frequency, confiding in her about things he hadn't shared with Sarah—his frustrations, his struggles, the loneliness he didn't know how to address at home. With Blaire, he felt understood in a way that didn't feel risky, or so he told himself.

Continued

One evening, Blaire suggested they meet up after work. It felt innocent enough, but as they talked over drinks, the chemistry between them grew undeniable. Seeking comfort in each other's presence, they ended up in David's car, where their friendship crossed a line he never imagined crossing. The rush of connection and relief he felt was fleeting, and almost immediately, David was overwhelmed by guilt and shame. The very thing he'd sought—a sense of ease, a release from his loneliness—had led him to a betrayal he couldn't undo.

Unable to live with the secret, David decided to confess to Sarah. His voice shook as he told her what had happened, bracing himself for her reaction. Sarah's devastation was palpable, her disbelief cutting through him as she struggled to comprehend why he'd turned to someone else instead of to her. She'd shared her grief with him, her vulnerability and hopes, only to discover that he'd sought solace in someone else's arms. "Why didn't you just tell me?" she asked, her voice thick with pain. David had no easy answer; he realized only then the extent to which he'd failed to let her in, choosing instead to nurse his sorrow in isolation and seek connection elsewhere. The chasm between them, once unspoken, now lay wide open, and David was left to confront the full impact of his choices.

David found himself grappling with layers of grief and regret, each one weighing heavily on him. The sadness over their failed attempts to start a family had been profound, a loss he hadn't fully acknowledged even to himself. But now, with the additional pain of his betrayal looming between them, he realized how much his own isolation and avoidance had compounded their struggles. He had been holding vigil not only over the grief of infertility but also over the pain he'd caused Sarah, a wound that grew deeper with each attempt to reach for solace outside their marriage.

Every day, David tried to show up for Sarah, yet he struggled with consistency. The magnitude of their losses and his guilt often left him emotionally overwhelmed, cycling between

Continued

moments of resolve and periods of doubt and self-blame. For Sarah, this inconsistency made it difficult to trust him again, and his efforts to reassure her often felt shaky and uncertain. She needed security and commitment from him, but David's own unresolved pain left him floundering, unable to provide the steady foundation they both needed.

He realized he'd have to learn how to hold space for both their hurts—his own grief, the guilt of his betrayal, and Sarah's shattered sense of safety. Therapy became a critical part of his journey, as he worked to face his pain and shame rather than evade them. Little by little, David began to see how his habitual withdrawal had only deepened the isolation they both felt. As he began to let Sarah in on his grief, not just as a partner but as someone with whom he could be vulnerable, he hoped to slowly rebuild a sense of safety in their relationship. It was a journey full of setbacks and painfully small steps, but David began to understand that his presence—consistent and open— was what would help heal the wounds he'd helped create.

Working with David and Sarah required a delicate balance—acknowledging each of their unique pains while helping them unify around shared goals for the future. Their journey was far from linear; at times because focusing on one person's pain would trigger unresolved hurt in the other, making it difficult to move forward. For David, every step toward healing his own wounds meant facing his guilt and shame head-on, while Sarah needed space to express her feelings of betrayal and loss without feeling responsible for managing David's responses. Initially, each attempt to honor their individual journeys felt like a fresh wound, reigniting old hurts and leaving both of them emotionally exposed.

In therapy, they learned to sit with each other's pain without letting it overshadow their own. This process was challenging, but it was essential. When David expressed his guilt or grief, Sarah learned to hold space for him, knowing that his remorse didn't diminish her hurt. Similarly, David

Continued

learned to listen to Sarah's feelings of betrayal without pulling away or attempting to fix things too quickly. This willingness to honor each other's journeys allowed them to build trust, brick by brick, in a way that hadn't been possible before.

Gradually, they began to move out of the crisis phase, where emotions ran high and everything felt like a potential rupture, and into a space where resilience became the center of their work. They grew better at recognizing their individual triggers and self-soothing, finding strength not only in their shared goals but also in the stability they were building within themselves. Their shared vision—of a life where they could support each other even in the toughest of times—became the foundation of their healing, a reminder of why they were doing this difficult work together. As they focused on cultivating resilience, David and Sarah began to feel the rewards of staying present with each other's pain and moving through it, rather than around it, toward a more unified and hopeful future.

WHAT DO THESE CASE STUDIES MEAN FOR ME?

The case studies I've shared illustrate how diverse the experiences of infidelity can be. From the emotional complexity of ongoing affairs to the transactional patterns of casual encounters, each man's story highlights unique challenges, emotions, and decisions. These examples also reveal the different ways couples navigate the recovery process. Whether it's the fear of exposure, the relief of discovery, or the raw vulnerability of starting therapy, each journey underscores that infidelity isn't one-size-fits-all, nor is it the path to healing.

Recovery, as these stories show, demands investment from both partners. The person who committed the betrayal must take accountability, explore their motivations, and lean into the discomfort of rebuilding trust. At the same time, the betrayed partner must engage in the hard work of processing pain, asking difficult questions, and exploring the broader dynamics of the relationship. When both partners commit to this work, they create the foundation for a more stable and successful future—one that isn't just about repairing what was broken but reimagining what's possible together.

Working with skilled therapists is a key part of this process. A talented therapist provides a safe and structured environment to navigate the tough conversations, address deep relational dynamics, and hold space for the difficult emotions that arise. Therapy isn't about finding a quick fix but about fostering genuine understanding and growth. While the road can be long and challenging, these case studies show that the outcomes are worth it. With effort, honesty, and the right support, couples can emerge stronger, more connected, and ready to face the future with intention and resilience.

The next chapter will explore recommendations I have for each partner to navigate the challenging road ahead.

9
▼

RECOMMENDATIONS

The path through infidelity recovery is far from linear. Every couple's journey is unique, with its own challenges, setbacks, and moments of growth. While it might be tempting to compare your experience to someone else's—especially if you've heard stories from friends, read articles, or seen examples in media—it's crucial to remember that what applies to others may not apply to you. No two relationships are the same, and infidelity doesn't play out in a predictable way. What works for one couple may not be the right fit for another, even if there are some overlapping themes or similar struggles.

STAY IN YOUR OWN STORY

One of the biggest challenges in the process of infidelity recovery is learning to stay within your own story. It's normal to seek advice or reassurance from others, but this can lead to unrealistic expectations if you assume their journey should mirror yours. Some couples may find forgiveness early on, while others spend years rebuilding trust. Some partners may feel intense anger for months, while others might feel numb or detached. Recovery isn't about following a prescribed path; it's about allowing space for each partner's unique emotions and navigating the ups and downs in a way that feels authentic to both of you.

It's also easy to fall into "should" thinking—believing you should be feeling a certain way, should have forgiven by now, or should have moved on because someone else did. Letting go of these comparisons allows you to focus on what you truly need to heal. This might mean going through difficult conversations multiple times, setting boundaries others might not understand, or finding support in places you didn't expect. By staying present in your own journey, you give yourself the permission to explore what recovery looks like for you, without the pressure of anyone else's expectations.

REMEMBER THAT EACH PARTNER IS SOLVING A DIFFERENT CHALLENGE

In infidelity recovery, it's essential to recognize that each partner experiences the pain of betrayal in very different ways and faces unique challenges as they navigate their emotions. The betraying partner may grapple with intense shame, guilt, and regret, often questioning their own self-worth and struggling with the impact of their actions on their partner. Meanwhile, the betrayed partner may experience a whirlwind of emotions—anger, sadness, confusion, and a profound sense of betrayal. Their reality has been shaken, and they're left to process a new understanding of their relationship. One of the greatest struggles for each partner—and one which is experienced uniquely— is the fracture infidelity gives to their identity. The man must reconcile that he is a man who did what he did. His partner must reconcile that she is a woman who was cheated on. The shifting identity challenge that each partner has to resolve is work that each partner has to do individually in order to move ahead. Each partner's pain is distinct, and acknowledging these differences is a key part of creating a supportive space for healing.

Beyond the infidelity itself, each partner also brings their own background, coping style, and emotional history into the recovery process. These differences shape how they react, how they seek comfort, and what they need to heal. One partner may find relief in talking things through repeatedly, while the other may need moments of quiet or physical reassurance instead. It's crucial to embrace this uniqueness, not only within the infidelity and recovery process but in each other as individuals. This means learning to respect the ways in which your partner processes emotions, even if it's unfamiliar or difficult to understand.

Understanding these unique needs fosters empathy, which is vital for moving forward. Rather than expecting each other to feel, respond, or heal in the same way, you open space for growth when you accept that your journeys are different yet intertwined. Recovery from infidelity asks each partner to honor those individual paths, finding ways to support each other without forcing conformity. This mutual respect allows both partners to feel valued for who they truly are, building a foundation of honesty and compassion that can strengthen the relationship in the long run.

FIND A THERAPIST TRAINED IN INFIDELITY RECOVERY

Finding a therapist who truly understands you and your partner is invaluable in the process of healing from infidelity. A strong connection with an individual therapist allows each partner to feel heard, safe, and supported as they work through their own unique experiences and emotional challenges. In addition to individual therapy, an experienced infidelity recovery couples therapist can help both partners communicate effectively, validate each other's pain, and begin to rebuild trust in a structured, balanced way. The quality of this therapeutic relationship is often what allows difficult conversations to happen and encourages each partner to keep engaging in the work.

Beyond individual and couples therapy, additional resources like supportive groups, couples retreats, pastoral counseling, or 12-step programs can offer valuable insights and a sense of community. These resources create opportunities to hear others' experiences, gain practical tools, and access a range of perspectives, each of which can be grounding. However, the key to maximizing these supports is ensuring they align and coordinate with the main therapeutic work. When therapists are able to collaborate and communicate—sharing the big-picture goals for each partner and for the relationship—there's less chance of conflicting messages or confusion. This coordination also helps each partner feel that they're moving toward a common understanding and reinforces a shared commitment to the healing process.

Coordinated care helps ensure that each partner's growth and understanding are continually building on one another. If, for instance, one partner's 12-step work focuses on accountability, that insight can directly inform how they approach communication in couples therapy. Meanwhile, if the other partner is processing their grief or rebuilding confidence, individual therapy can help them prepare for the shared challenges in couples sessions. This integrative approach supports a comprehensive, sustainable path forward, one in which each partner is both individually fulfilled and jointly engaged in a hopeful future.

REMEMBER THAT HEALING TAKES TIME

Patience is perhaps one of the most critical elements in the journey of infidelity recovery. This work is complex, challenging, and emotionally intense, and it is rarely fast. Both partners are often carrying raw, painful emotions, and progress can feel agonizingly slow. Resiliency, the ability to withstand and adapt through hardship, is essential but doesn't appear overnight—it is cultivated gradually. True recovery is not about sweeping the past away quickly but about facing it fully, understanding it, and, ultimately, transforming the relationship in a way that feels genuine and sustainable.

In times of uncertainty, patience becomes a lifeline. When you're unsure whether you'll stay or go, committing to the process in small increments can be incredibly grounding. Taking it 30, 60, or 90 days at a time allows each partner to be present in the work without the pressure of a final decision hanging over every conversation. It also creates space to observe shifts—no matter how small—in the relationship. Promise to stay in the work for that chosen timeframe, without the looming threat of departure, and see if any progress begins to emerge. This approach can reduce some of the panic and defensiveness that arise in the immediate aftermath of infidelity, enabling both partners to focus on building, or rebuilding, the skills that will help them navigate together.

The promise here is not forever; it's a promise to commit to exploration and honesty in the immediate present. Giving yourselves these windows of time encourages openness and provides enough structure to see if reconnection or positive changes are possible. This patience-driven approach is a compassionate way to hold space for hope and healing, allowing both partners to recognize what is evolving within themselves and each other. It also acknowledges that growth is often incremental, with each period offering new insights and gradually building the resiliency needed to face the next stage of recovery.

THE HEALTHIEST RELATIONSHIPS HAVE THE CLEAREST BOUNDARIES

Setting boundaries is essential in navigating infidelity recovery. Deciding who will know the details of the infidelity—whether friends, family, or even social circles—fundamentally shapes the recovery journey. The more people who know about the infidelity, the more opinions, advice, and judgments will inevitably surround you, adding layers of external expectations and potentially intensifying your own confusion. While these people may be well-intentioned, they may inadvertently pressure you and your partner to make choices that align with their beliefs rather than your unique needs. As the recovery unfolds, this external involvement can create a sense of obligation, where you feel compelled to manage not only your healing but also the expectations and opinions of others.

Having a few trusted people who can genuinely offer support without crossing boundaries or inserting themselves into the relationship is invaluable. These confidants can provide a safe space for you to process emotions, offer grounding perspectives, and encourage growth without judgment. However, broadcasting your situation widely is usually counterproductive, making it harder to keep the focus on your and your partner's needs. Navigating recovery is complex and emotionally taxing as it is; adding external "noise" can make it even more overwhelming.

Choose your support carefully, ideally people who can hold emotional boundaries, respect your decisions, and not bring personal agendas into your recovery process. Boundaries are not about isolation but about protecting the sanctity of the work you and your partner are doing. It's your story and managing how and when to share it helps keep the focus on what matters: moving forward together in a way that feels right for both of you.

Establishing boundaries around behaviors and interactions is another crucial part of infidelity recovery. These boundaries define how you'll navigate physical closeness, communication, and mutual expectations during this time of healing. If you're not sharing the same living space, for instance, discuss what conditions would need to be met to allow a return. Similarly, if touch or physical intimacy has been halted, explore what each partner would need to feel comfortable reintroducing touch, even in small gestures. Determining these behavioral boundaries creates a roadmap for rebuilding connection gradually, respecting each person's comfort and safety.

Communication around the pain itself also requires boundaries. Consider when and how you'll discuss painful topics, aiming for times when both of you are prepared to engage constructively. It's also essential to agree on the consistency of therapy—both individually and as a couple—to ensure the work is ongoing and not left as an "optional" part of recovery.

Reoffending boundaries are also critical. What are the consequences, and how will you hold each other accountable to avoid repeating old patterns? Boundaries around honesty and the handling of painful details are especially complex, balancing the need for transparency with each person's emotional tolerance.

These are deeply personal negotiations that, while uncomfortable, lay a foundation for mutual respect and security. Therapy offers a structured, safe environment to help navigate these challenging conversations. It provides an external perspective, helping both partners articulate needs, define boundaries, and build agreements that honor both voices.

Maintain a Focus on Self-Care

Self-care is a cornerstone of infidelity recovery, and it can take many forms—each unique to the individual. While the pain may feel overwhelming, looking to your partner to remove or heal all of it is unrealistic and places an unsustainable burden on the relationship. This journey requires each person to own their own healing, even if the work was not something they ever wanted or expected to take on. Self-care, while challenging to prioritize in a time of crisis, provides the foundation upon which recovery rests.

Self-care might involve reconnecting with activities that bring you comfort or joy, establishing routines to regain stability, or setting aside time for reflection. It can mean engaging in practices like meditation, exercise, journaling, or spending time with supportive friends who offer a nonjudgmental ear. For many, self-care also involves cultivating a compassionate inner voice—reminding oneself that healing from betrayal is hard work and that setbacks and difficult emotions are normal.

It's also important to recognize that while your partner can offer support, true healing is ultimately an internal process. Taking responsibility for your own well-being ensures that you're not just moving through the recovery process but doing so in a way that builds resilience and self-trust. This personal growth strengthens not only the individual but also the relationship, creating a more solid foundation for rebuilding trust and connection.

Embarking on the journey of infidelity recovery is a commitment that, once begun, needs to be seen through—whether that leads to staying together or ultimately parting ways. This work, painful and demanding as it may be, is not just about the present relationship but about each partner's future self. Without tending to the pain and injury left by betrayal, we carry unhealed wounds forward, coloring future connections and repeating cycles we may not fully understand. The question becomes, does this relationship mean enough to do the work together, or will you find that path separately?

Doing the work together requires courage, patience, and willingness to face hard truths alongside one another. There will be missteps, moments of emotional turmoil that are unexpected, and fears of backsliding. Healing together demands mutual vulnerability, the ability to rebuild trust brick by brick, and the acceptance that real change unfolds slowly. If this relationship still holds value, what will it take to transform it into one that is stronger, healthier, and deeply honest? This is the kind of resilience that, once cultivated, becomes a lifelong strength for each person involved.

Healing, while difficult, only grows more challenging when postponed. Facing this process now, with intention, curiosity, and courage, gives each of you the best chance to emerge on the other side with greater clarity, resilience, and perhaps even a renewed commitment to love—whether in this relationship or the next. Again, as my grandmother Anna wisely put it, "Do your work now, or do your work later … eventually, you will have to do the work, and the longer you wait, the harder it is."

REFERENCES

Braun-Harvey, Douglas, and Michael A. Vigorito. *Treating Out of Control Sexual Behavior: Rethinking Sex Addiction.* Springer Publishing Company, 2015.

Cann, Arnie, Jessica L. Mangum, and Marissa Wells. "Distress in Response to Relationship Infidelity: The Roles of Gender and Attitudes About Relationships." *Journal of Sex Research* 38, no. 3 (2001): 185-190.

Clarke, Victoria, Virginia Braun, and Kate Wooles. "Thou Shalt Not Covet Another Man? Exploring Constructions of Same-Sex and Different-Sex Infidelity Using Story Completion." *Journal of Community & Applied Social Psychology* 25, no. 2 (2015): 153-166.

Connell, R. W. "Studying Men and Masculinity." *Resources for Feminist Research* 29, nos. 1/2 (2002): 43-55.

Connell, R. W., and James W. Messerschmidt "Hegemonic Masculinity: Rethinking the Concept." *Gender and Society* 19, no. 6 (2005): 829-859.

Crenshaw, Kimberlé. "Demarginalizing the Intersection of Race and Sex: A Black Feminist Critique of Antidiscrimination Doctrine, Feminist Theory, and Antiracist Politics." *University of Chicago Forum* 1, no. 8 (1989).

Crenshaw, Theresa L. *The Alchemy of Love and Lust: How Our Sex Hormones Influence Our Relationships.* Gallery Books, 1997.

Curry, Tommy J. *The Man-Not: Race, Class, Genre, and Dilemmas of Black Manhood.* Temple University Press, 2017.

Davis, Porter. *Handbook for Husbands (and Wives): A Complete Guide for Sexual Adjustment in Marriage.* Banner Books, 1949.

DeMaris, Alfred. "Distal and Proximal Influences on the Risk of Extramarital Sex: A Prospective Study of Longer Duration Marriages." *Journal of Sex Research,* 46, no. 6 (2009): 597-607.

Fincham, Frank D., and Steven R. H. Beach. "Marriage in the New Millennium: A Decade in Review." *National Council on Family Relations* 72, no. 343 (2010): 630-649.

Haltzman, Scott. *The Secrets of Surviving Infidelity.* Johns Hopkins University Press, 2013.

hooks, bell. *The Will to Change: Men, Masculinity, and Love.* Washington Square Press, 2004.

Kronenfeld, Elliott. "Implications of Infidelity: A Discourse Analysis of Disenfranchised Grief Experienced by Men in Therapy for Infidelity Recovery." PhD. diss., California Institute of Integral Studies, 2020. Proquest (28489912).

Kronenfeld, Elliott. *Couples by Intention: Creating and Cultivating Relationships that Matter!* SDP Publishing, 2018.

Lusterman, Don-David. "Marital Infidelity: The Effects of Delayed Traumatic Reaction." In *Handbook of the Clinical Treatment of Infidelity,* edited by Fred P. Piercy, Katherine M. Hertlein, and Joseph L. Wetchler. Routledge, 2011.

Pascoe, Cheri Jo. *Dude, You're a Fag: Masculinity and Sexuality in High School.* University of California Press, 2012

Piercy, Fred P., Katherine M. Hertlein, and Joseph L. Wetchler. "Infidelity: An Overview." In *Handbook of the Clinical Treatment of Infidelity,* edited by Fred P. Piercy, Katherine M. Hertlein, and Joseph L. Wetchler. Routledge, 2011.

Sprecher, Susan. "Social Exchange Theories and Sexuality." *Journal of Sex Research* 35, no.1 (1998): 32-43.

Treger, Stanislav, and Sprecher, Susan. "The Influences of Sociosexuality and Attachment Style on Reactions to Emotional versus Sexual Infidelity." *Journal of Sex Research* 48, no. 5 (2011): 413-422.

Ward, Jane. *Not Gay: Sex Between Straight White Men.* NYU Press, 2015.

Zapien, Nicolle. *Clinical Treatment Directions for Infidelity: A Phenomenological Framework for Understanding.* Routledge, 2018.

ABOUT THE AUTHOR

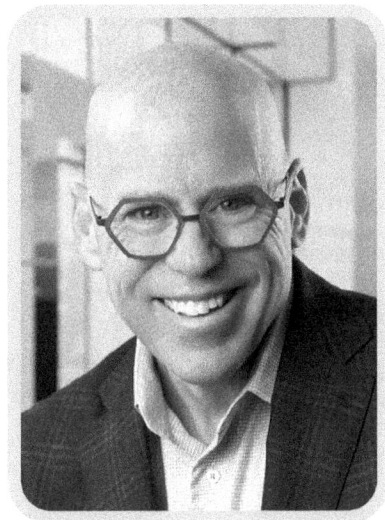

DR. KRONENFELD is an internationally known author, sex therapist, educator, TEDx speaker, and yoga teacher. His work has focused on helping people find, maintain, and grow their best relationships even when faced with the challenges of infertility, infidelity, challenged intimacy, parenting, and other complex life situations. He is a frequent guest on podcasts and other media outlets, talking about the realities of relationships. As a university educator, he teaches sex and gender in China and the U.S. at the master's and doctoral levels. Elliott is often on the road giving keynote talks and lectures at government agencies, universities, national organizations, conferences, and private practices on topics that relate to the human experience. A lover of travel, Elliott has been on every continent and brings his cultural experience and sensitivity to his work because he believes the human experience has commonality and uniqueness at the same time. He currently lives in Maine with his family where he is a yoga practitioner and is constantly planning his next journey somewhere across the globe.

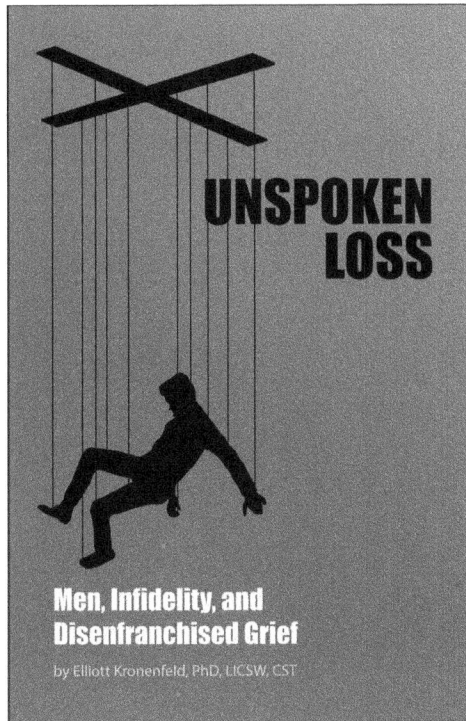

UNSPOKEN LOSS: MEN, INFIDELITY, AND DISENFRANCHISED GRIEF

Dr. Elliott Kronenfeld, LICSW, CSTS

www.unspoken-loss.com

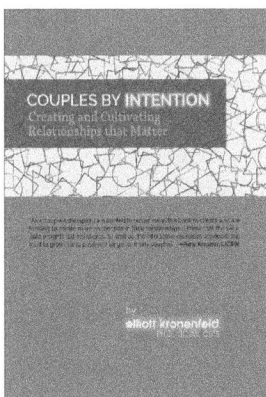

Publisher: SDP Publishing
Also available in ebook format

Also by the author:
Couples by Intention

TO PURCHASE:

SDP Publishing.com
Barnes & Noble.com
Amazon.com

Available at all major bookstores

SDP Publishing

www.SDPPublishing.com
Contact us at: info@SDPPublishing.com

www.ingramcontent.com/pod-product-compliance
Lightning Source LLC
Chambersburg PA
CBHW051424090426
42737CB00014B/2812